2020 年安徽省级新文科、新医科研究与改革实践项目
（2020wyxm038）

安徽省级"六卓越、一拔尖"卓越人才培养创新
项目（2020zyrc034）

2022 年安徽工程大学校级科研项目"基于'二语动机
自我系统'理论框架下的动机策略研究"（Xjky2022212，
Xjky2022214）

安徽工程大学重点教学研究项目"基于 SPOC 的大学英
语课程思政教学设计研究"（2021jyxm18）

大学英语动态动机教学模式研究

A Study of a Dynamic Motivational Teaching Model in the Chinese College English Context

王钰 著

浙江工商大学出版社
ZHEJIANG GONGSHANG UNIVERSITY PRESS
·杭州·

图书在版编目(CIP)数据

大学英语动态动机教学模式研究 / 王钰著. — 杭州：浙江工商大学出版社，2022.11
ISBN 978-7-5178-5128-8

Ⅰ．①大… Ⅱ．①王… Ⅲ．①英语－教学模式－研究－高等学校 Ⅳ．①H319.3

中国版本图书馆CIP数据核字(2022)第172638号

大学英语动态动机教学模式研究
DAXUE YINGYU DONGTAI DONGJI JIAOXUE MOSHI YANJIU
王钰 著

责任编辑	张莉娅
责任校对	鲁燕青
封面设计	张　瑜
责任印制	包建辉
出版发行	浙江工商大学出版社
	（杭州市教工路198号　邮政编码310012）
	（E-mail：zjgsupress@163.com）
	（网址：http://www.zjgsupress.com）
	电话：0571-88904980，88831806（传真）
排　　版	杭州彩地电脑图文有限公司
印　　刷	杭州宏雅印刷有限公司
开　　本	710mm×1000mm 1/16
印　　张	16
字　　数	268千
版 印 次	2022年11月第1版　2022年11月第1次印刷
书　　号	ISBN 978-7-5178-5128-8
定　　价	65.00元

Foreword

The purpose of this experimental study was to examine the effects of the dynamic motivational model on college students' motivation toward English as a foreign language, students' language learning, and the academic achievements of students of the high, medium and low English levels in a heterogeneous class. Lasting one semester, the quasi-experimental teaching program began from September, 2020 and extended to January, 2021. The participants involved in this study consisted of 142 non-English majors from a provincial key university in China. The experimental group included 72 participants, who were treated with the dynamic motivational teaching model, and the control group contained 73 participants, who were taught with the traditional teaching method. Both quantitative and qualitative methods were employed in this research to achieve methodological triangulation. The quantitative study contained motivational questionnaires, two oral tests and two written tests, and the qualitative data included students' twice self-reports. Descriptive Analysis, Independent Samples Test and Paired Samples Test were utilized to make between- and within-group comparison and see if there were significant differences between the two groups.

The results of the study showed that the students under the dynamic motivational teaching model demonstrated a stronger motivation to learn English than those in the control group. The students' self-reports indicated that learners enjoyed the learning atmosphere and became more confident under such motivational teaching model. In addition, the dynamic motivational teaching model helped to develop learners' general English proficiency after one semester's motivational teaching treatment, the experimental group achieved as well as the control group in the receptive knowledge (reading, listening), but the former was far superior to the latter in the productive knowledge (speaking, translation, composition). Furthermore, the findings on the effects of the teaching model on learners with different initial levels of English achievement suggested that it was effective for high achievers in improving their overall English proficiency. While for medium- and low-achievers the dynamic motivational teaching model helped enhance their oral communicative competence and writing ability. The traditional teaching model was effective only in the written test score of the low achievers.

The major findings of this study suggest that the dynamic motivational teaching model is an effective way to contribute to the enhancement of the college freshmen's motivation toward learning as a foreign language and the development of their target language proficiency. Finally, pedagogical implications, limitation and recommendation for the application of the dynamic motivational teaching model in foreign language teaching are also proposed.

CONTENTS

Chapter 1　Introduction

Chapter 2　Review of Related Literature

Chapter 3 Research Methodology

Chapter 4 Research Findings

Chapter 5 Conclusion, Discussion, and Recommendation

List of Tables

List of Figures

Chapter 1 Introduction

This chapter provides a research space by presenting an insightful research background, rationale, research questions, objectives of the study, followed by the theoretical framework and conceptual framework. Then, scope of the study, definition of terms and significance of the study are also elaborated. Finally, Chapter 1 ends up with the summary and the structure of the book.

1.1 Background of the Study

The problem of teaching college freshmen students always haunts college English teachers in China. Because of the fierce competition in the entrance examination, most students in high school have to do their utmost to be enrolled in a university. The problem is that once the students enter a college, they tend to regard it as their ultimate goal. Many students find themselves losing passion in continually devoting themselves to studying in college, and this has been confirmed by Cai (2010) in his survey conducted among 1,282 teachers from 289 universities that 42.8 percent of teachers complain that their students are demotivated in college English learning.

Motivation, defined as the impetus to create and sustain intentions and goal-seeking acts (Ames, 1989), is a term that cannot be overemphasized in English learning, because it determines to what extent a learner is willing to involve in an activity and his or her attitude towards English learning. It influences learners' autonomy, attention, effort, persistence, and the frequency of using learning strategies. In a word, it plays an important role in determining success or failure in any learning situation. Considering the common learning burnout and deficit in motivation among students, it is imperative for teachers to take some measures and use effective strategies to help students to overcome this negative phenomenon and regain their driving force for learning English.

The focus of students' motivation and active learning is also a requirement of Ministry of Education of the People's Republic of China. According to the College English Teaching Requirement (2007), a new teaching mode should be adopted in college English teaching which should be beneficial to arouse the enthusiasm of both teachers and students, especially to reflect the main position of the students and the leading role of the teachers in the teaching process. Among them, "arousing the enthusiasm of the students" and "reflecting the main position of the students in the teaching process" are to stimulate the students' English learning motivation and promote their active learning. Accordingly, an important aspect of "arousing the enthusiasm of teachers" and "embodying the leading role of teachers in the teaching process" is to make teachers consciously adopt various strategies and give full play to the role of encouraging students to learn. It can be seen that the current college English teaching in China should not only emphasize how to impart students' English knowledge and skills, but also cultivate students' interest in English learning and strengthen their English learning motivation, i.e. the teacher should direct from "how to teach" to "how to motivate".

The increasing understanding of the importance of motivation boosted a wealth of pedagogical implication in educational context as to how second language (L2) teacher can intervene to promote learners' L2 motivation in terms of motivational strategies (Dörnyei, 2001; Dörnyei & Malderez, 1997; Williams & Burden, 1997). The most comprehensive practical framework of motivational strategies is provided by Dörnyei (2001) via Motivational

Teaching Practice in the L2 Classrooms, with which, as suggested by Dörnyei, L2 teachers can be equipped with the capability to stimulate learners' motivation and help them maintain their motivation throughout their L2 learning process. However, as research findings (Guilloteaux & Dörnyei, 2008) have revealed that the teacher's use of motivational strategies in foreign language teaching will involve not merely choosing a "bag of tricks" in the form of a few motivational strategies, but also embed these in a more generally motivating L2 teaching approach to take into consideration the students' desire for more interesting lessons.

With complex and dynamic processes, the motivation involves a multitude of personal characteristics, beliefs, and perceptions fluctuating over time and circumstances (Kaplan A. et al., 2019). Motivation psychologists have long been concerned about how to better understand why individuals behave or think the way they do, what drives a person towards specific choices and actions, and what moves them to work hard and stick to these actions (Erdil, 2016). Reflected in L2 pedagogical implication, motivational teaching can not afford to focus on only a certain single construct with the intention of generating and maintaining learners' motivation, and to achieve a maximized effect. A combining effort of motivational variables from different aspects in the teaching process must be made to deal with the rich, multi-construct, contextualized motivational system.

1.2 Rationale

Despite the increasingly frequent interaction among different countries in the world and learning English has become more and more important as a foreign language, lack of motivation still remains as one of the biggest challenges in English as a Foreign Language (EFL) classrooms in China. When delving into what factors led to students' lack of motivation, several research findings on L2 motivation targeted Chinese freshmen (Xu, 2018; Cao, 2018) have pointed to the students' negative perceptions of classroom practices, among which the teachers' teaching method and teaching style are among the most to blame. Actually, although many students have passed their English college entrance exam with high scores, they are found to have developed so-called "mute English", that is, with a good mastery of language rules and vocabulary, but are weak in listening comprehension and speaking due to limited experience of communication. This can at least be partially attributed to the traditional means of language teaching. In China, most language classrooms are still text-centered and input-based (Wen, 2015). That is to say, the textbook, which is supposed to be mediate for students to learn has turned out to be the core to organize listening and reading activities, and students learn a foreign language only for the purpose of memorizing vocabulary, sentence patterns, grammar, etc. The whole learning process becomes "input" of the language elements and rules of a foreign language. Generally, there are two typical Chinese traditional teaching modes (Wen, 2015): bottom-up, during which the teacher focuses on language points with no larger structures for meaningful communications; and top-down, where meaning is what teachers care with no conditions for learners to use what they learn. No matter in which way, most college English teachers in China pay more attention to teaching than using and to language knowledge than to language communicative competence. The consequence of such teaching mode is, on the one hand, the separation of learning and using and low efficiency of teaching lead to the severe deficiency of college students' ability in the language production and fail to meet the demand of their future career and the society as a whole; on the other hand, with almost a decade's experience of exam-oriented English learning, college freshmen often have more than enough receptive and inertial English knowledge. If the college English teaching still follows the middle school English learning model with continual input and limited using English for communication, the students may suffer from "indigestion", the lack of appetite for any input "delicacies", which will inevitably lead to "anorexia" . It is under such circumstance that Chinese distinguished scholar Wen Qiufang (2015) puts forward the "Production-Oriented Approach" (POA), with a core idea that to learn a foreign language is to use it. Unlike traditional Chinese teaching which emphasizes learning rather than using or the Western task-based or project-based approaches focusing on practicing with insufficient instruction, the POA starts teaching with language production and ends with production while input serves as a core to help accomplish productive activities. It advocates the teaching idea of "learning and using as an integral whole", using output activities not only as the driving force to stimulate students' enthusiasm for learning, but also as teaching objectives, and input activities as the enabling means to help students achieve the goal. In this study, the POA was adopted to be its teaching method to take the following two reasons into consideration: First, adult college students love goal-driven and problem-solving learning (Wen, 2017). Second, since it was created in 2007, the last years have witnessed the tremendous popularity of this teaching method and English teachers' immense enthusiasm in applying it into the English teaching practice. Many experiments conducted by researchers and scholars have proved the POA's advantages in comparison to traditional methods. For example, during one semester of empirical study, Zhang (2017) finds out that this teaching method has noticeable strength in increasing students' learning interest, as well as improving their L2 learning motivation.

In order to transform the traditional teaching style where teachers are the centre of teaching and students passive recipient, leaving the language learner with seldom room for involvement and participation, and students are easily getting bored, which leads to the decline of their motivation to learn English, this teaching model adopts cooperative learning as the teaching organization technique out of the following considerations: (1) In the framework of process-oriented motivational strategies developed by Dörnyei (2001) in his motivational teaching practice, the first key unit is "creating the basic motivational conditions", which mainly refers to creating a pleasant and supportive atmosphere in the classroom and a cohesive learner group with appropriate group norms. Previous studies (Davis, 1997; Brown, 2001) have proved that the interaction provides learners with more opportunities to use the target language, reduces learners' anxiety and makes them more confident. (2) Compared with teacher-led classroom learning, learners in the group are more involved in "conversational correction" (Doughty & Pica, 1986) or meaning communication (Long, 1996), which can make the input obtained by students easier to understand and thus promote second language acquisition. (3) It has built a supportive and less threatening learning environment, so as to create an optimal schooling experience for college students. (4) It has increased the rate of learning retention.

This teaching model utilizes multimodality as its teaching means, because learners are more motivated to learn the language if they think it is interesting and useful. If teachers explain the text mainly relying on the oral explanation, students will get bored easily and cannot concentrate themselves for certain long in the class. Besides, different students have different learning styles, while some find it is the listening material that makes them remember easily, some will never forget what they have seen if it is in the form of an art picture. Implying in pedagogy, modern pedagogy believes that pictures, videos, colors and many other sorts of multimodalities can be combined to give students a rich and alternative stimulus to the sense organs and set a lively and plump teaching context. It can provide learners with multi-sensory experience, and can stimulate students' enthusiasm and interest in participating in learning and communication. So, the oral and written input in the teaching should be in a variety of forms to adapt to students with different learning characteristics.

Motivation has been considered one of the key components for successful L2 learning. The last few decades have seen a plethora of L2 motivation research which began with the psycho-social patterns of Robert Gardner and Wallace Lambert in the late 1950s (Gardner & Lambert, 1959; Gardner, 1985), followed by cognitive context pattern (Crookes & Schmidt, 1991; Deci E. L., 2004), process-oriented framework (Dörnyei, 2005; Dörnyei & Ushioda, 2009), and further developed by the socio-dynamic perspectives (Dörnyei & Ushioda, 2011) and the latest direct motivation currents (Dörnyei, Kubanyiova, 2014; Dörnyei, Ibrahim, Muir, 2015). However, most of the studies have been directed at internal structural characteristics and theoretical model construction of motivation and motivational strategies. In order to offer pedagogical implications in the context of L2 learning, Dörnyei (2001) suggests a framework of motivational strategy for L2 instructors to use in class: Motivational Teaching Practice. Later on, in an attempt to grasp the complex characteristic of language learning motivation from a different perspective, Dörnyei (2005, 2009) reconceptualizes language learning motivation with the L2 Motivational Self System (L2MSS) framework combined with a self and identity theory. Many empirical researches have confirmed its effectiveness in providing a more explanatory power for L2 learning motivation. Hence, this study has utilized these two theoretical frameworks as the guide.

Although teaching method, teaching organization and teaching means are crucial in teaching practice in general, they have not yet been considered to be associated with one another for increasing L2 motivational learning. In addition, despite the fact that the motivational strategies represented here by Motivational Teaching Practice and L2MSS were proved to be able to help teachers to enhance the L2 learners' motivation, they can never be used in vacuum, but have to be woven into the contents and processes of

L2 instruction (Guilloteaux & Dörnyei, 2008). Furthermore, although the last decades have seen a considerable amount of research conducted on L2 learning motivation and classroom practices to increase students' motivation and has yielded many motivation theories and models, to be teacher-friendly, there is a need for a systematic and unified model to transfer knowledge of motivation into heightening motivating practices in the context of second language learning classroom. Teaching a language is a multidimensional task which requires the combining efforts of teaching elements to meet the needs of a classroom with various levels of proficiency in learning a foreign language. Therefore, this study here has combined the three crucial teaching components with motivation strategies into a dynamic framework in order to systematically function on the intensity of students' L2 motivation in a pleasant and stimulating setting. Motivation is much more intricate and complex than a single teaching element would allow, therefore, it is necessary to make use of and bring into full play various methods and techniques which will minimize the differences within a classroom and help learners to participate in and benefit from the lessons equally. Just as the complexity and multidimensional nature of L2 learning motivation call for different approaches to understand it, so generating and maintaining the L2 motivation also need the interplay of a multitude of motivational variables in language teaching process. It is believed that if the classroom can be turned into a place where students like to stay because the content is interesting and closely related to their current and future study and career, where the learning goals are challenging yet manageable, and the atmosphere is enjoyable and supportive, it is more likely to expect an enhanced students' L2 learning motivation.

1.3 Research Questions

The researcher has attempted to develop a dynamic motivational teaching model in the Chinese college English context. This book mainly discusses the following three research questions in a comprehensive and systematic way:

Q1. What are the effects of the dynamic motivational teaching model on learners' motivation toward learning English as a foreign language?

Q2. What are the effects of the dynamic motivational teaching model on the improvement of the EFL learners' English proficiency?

Q3. What are the effects of the dynamic motivational teaching model on the high/medium/low English academic achievers in a heterogeneous class?

1.4 Research Objectives

The objective of this research is to create an ideally dynamic model of English classroom teaching in the Chinese college English context. Through the interplay of motivational teaching contextual factors and motivational strategies, this dynamic teaching model is intended to maximize the likelihood of students' L2 learning motivation, which in turn can be transformed into action in the L2 classroom setting and improve L2 language proficiency. To be specific, this study aims:

(1) To investigate the effectiveness of the dynamic motivational teaching model on learners' motivation toward learning English as a foreign language;

(2) To find out the effectiveness of the dynamic motivational teaching model on the improvement of the EFL learners' language proficiency;

(3) To study the effectiveness of the dynamic motivational teaching model on the high/medium/low achievers in a heterogeneous class.

1.5 Theoretical Framework

In order to deal with the multifaceted nature of language learning motivation from a blended and integrative perspective, this study proposes to construct a dynamic motivational teaching model in the Chinese college

English through a multitude of motivational variables in language teaching. The theoretical framework for the current study is based on Motivational Teaching Practice in the L2 Classrooms (Dörnyei, 2001), L2 Motivational Self System (Dörnyei, 2005, 2009), Production-Oriented Approach (Wen, 2015), Collaborative Learning and Multimodal Teaching.

Traditionally, motivational psychologists have been more concerned about what motivation is than about how we can use this knowledge to motivate learners. Recently, however, there has been a marked change, and more and more researchers have decided to look at the pedagogical implications of research by conceptualizing motivational strategies. Motivational strategies refer to instructional interventions consciously applied by teachers to elicit and stimulate students' motivation, or self-regulating strategies that are used purposefully by individual students to manage the level of their own motivation. The motivational strategies discussed here belong to the first type, namely, the instructional techniques used by teachers. A survey of the educational psychology literature related to the study of motivation in the classroom reveals many publications on teachers' behaviors that should be effective in fostering students' motivation in the classroom. Yet, it also reveals the absence of a theory-based framework that can accommodate the diverse behaviors, though Dörnyei (2001) is a notable exception in the L2 field.

His theoretical framework for a motivational L2 teaching practice comprises four main dimensions, which are further broken down into over 100 motivational techniques:

• Creating the basic motivational conditions, namely, laying the foundations of motivation through establishing a good teacher-student rapport, a pleasant and supportive classroom atmosphere, and a cohesive learner group with appropriate group norms.

• Generating initial motivation, that is, "whetting the students' appetite" by using strategies designed to develop positive attitudes toward the language course and language learning in general, and to increase the learners' expectancy of success.

• Maintaining and protecting motivation through promoting situation-specific task motivation (e.g. by designing stimulating, enjoyable, and relevant tasks), by providing learners with experiences of success, by allowing them to maintain a positive social image even during the often face-threatening task of having to communicate with a severely limited language code, and finally, by promoting learners' autonomy.

• Encouraging positive retrospective self-evaluation through the promotion of adaptive attributions and the provision of effective and encouraging feedbacks, as well as by increasing learners' satisfaction and by offering grades in a motivational manner.

Later on, based on the achievements of the psychological school and the sociocultural school, Dörnyei (2005, 2009) further promotes and deepens the study of motivation theory, and puts forward a new theoretical framework having a substantial impact on L2 motivation, namely "L2 Motivational Self-System". As the latest approach to L2 motivation, it has proved an internationally acknowledge valid approach to L2 motivation and has demonstrated a powerful explanation in L2 achievement in different EFL contexts (Taguchi, Magid, Papi, 2009; Csizér & Kormos, 2009; Thompson & Erdil-Moody, 2014).

This theoretical framework consists of "ideal L2 self", "ought-to L2 self", and "L2 learning experience". "Ideal L2 self" refers to all the L2-related features that a person desires and hopes to have, thus a person with an ideal L2 self-image in mind with a high L2 achiever will have a strong stimulus to become the ideal L2 self. While "ought-to L2 self", refers to the degree to which the learner thinks he should reach, in order to achieve the expectations of others or to avoid negative outcomes. "L2 learning experience" refers to the learner's specific learning experience associated with a specific learning situation, such as a teacher, curriculum, or peer group. The basic assumption of the theoretical system is, if a proficient user of the target language is an ideal/ought to be part of the learner's self, he will have a strong motivation to learn the target language, because he has the desire to close the gap between the real self and the possible self.

The L2 motivational self-system provides a new approach to understand language learning motivation. An important component of this theory is the learners' vision of themselves in a future state. By using the powerful function of imagination, that is, directing students to create an attractive vision of their ideal language self, it opens a new avenue for promoting students' motivation. Dörnyei put forward several classroom activities to enhance the vision and six components in his motivational framework, that is, construction of the ideal L2 self, imagery enhancement, making the ideal L2 self plausible, developing an action plan, activating the ideal L2 self and considering failure.

While there have been many researches on L2 motivation indicating the positive relevance of teachers' use of motivational strategies for promoting motivation in L2 foreign language classrooms, the best motivational intervention is simply to improve the quality of our teaching (Dörnyei, 2001). That is to say, to optimize the learning outcome, the motivational practices have to be blended into an effective L2 instruction, which comprises the teaching method, teaching organization and teaching means in this study.

Motivated by the aspiration to enhance the quality of foreign teaching in China, the POA has been proven to be a very promising pedagogy of English teaching with Chinese characteristics. Combining the perspective of curriculum theory and second language acquisition theory, and based on Krashen's (1985) input hypothesis and Swain's (1995) output hypothesis , the POA advocates the concept of "learning for using" and "learning promoting using", using output as the driving force to prompt students to learn, and the input as the means to help students from being less to more capable. Both are significant and interdependent with each other. Specifically speaking, the teacher creates a communicative scenario, assigns students output task and lets them try out to produce before the class. On the one hand, students can know the communicative value of the task, but on the other hand, they can realize what they lack from performing these activities, thus creating a desire to learn. Then it is what the second phase enabling is for, when the teacher provides input materials, designs the teaching procedure carefully, and guides students to learn selectively and gradually what is useful to help them to accomplish the productive activities.

The overall framework of the POA consists of three parts: teaching concept, teaching hypothesis and teaching process. The first part "teaching concept" consists of the principles of "learning-centered", "learning-using integration", and "whole-person education" and is the guiding ideology of the second and the third parts, which determines the direction and overall goal of classroom teaching. The second part "teaching hypothesis" includes "output-driven", "input-enabling", and "selective learning" and serves the theoretical basis of each link of classroom teaching, which needs to be tested one by one. The third part "teaching process" which contains motivating, enabling, and assessing is the carrier of realizing "teaching idea" and testing "teaching hypothesis", and it is also the step and means to realize the teaching goal of the POA.

Collaborative learning refers to the learning activities of students engaged in groups as the basic units in the teaching process. Originated in the US since the early 1970s, it has become one of the most successful models of contemporary teaching reform, attracting much attention from researchers and educators (Slavin, 1995; Wang, 2011). Emphasizing student-centered and teacher-led, and through the cooperation and interaction between teacher and students, students and students, this learning strategy promotes group members to achieve the goal of learning from each other and completing tasks together, so as to obtain the individual and collective learning performance. Johnson & Johnson (1999) note, "Collaborative learning is the use of group forms in teaching where students work together to maximize themselves and learning for others." Smith et al., (2005) believe that collaborative learning could not only improve learners' cognitive ability, but also promote its non-cognitive development. A great number of studies have shown that collaborative learning is effective in improving the classroom's atmosphere and students' psychological state, and plays a positive role in promoting the learners' academic performance, practical ability, and social ability (Jensen et al., 2002; Li, 2007; Xiao & Qiong, 2014; Cao & Bai, 2018). The characteristics of collaborative learning are (1) positive interdependence, (2) promotive interaction, (3) individual accountability, (4) interpersonal and small group skills, and (5) group processing. In collaborative learning, there are many collaborative learning techniques that can be used to help teachers organize teaching and learning in and outside classroom, and the methods adopted in this study are Three-Step Interview, Think-Pair-Share, Student Team Achievement Division (STAD), and Adapted Jigsaw Reading.

Multimodal discourse refers to the use of hearing, vision, touch and other senses, and through language, image, sound, action and other means and symbolic resources to conduct communication. (Zhang, 2009) One of the most basic concepts of developing modern multimedia technology is that multimodal communication can enable recipients to obtain information through multi-channel, and therefore help them to understand and memorize better than a single channel discourse. For example, PPT can provide text, voice, graphics, image, video through visual and auditory sensations. Although the L2 classroom is not a real social communication environment, multimedia technology, such as image, video, audio, etc., can provide it with a context as real as possible. For example, the authentic video material obtained from the real communication scene can make the context knowledge more specific and enable students to understand better. Multi-channel information jointly stimulates the individual cerebral cortex of learners and can trigger a stronger reaction than a single information channel, and therefore can be more conducive for individuals to process and memorize the information.

It is based on the three teaching contextual factors and two types of motivational strategies discussed above that this study establish its motivation-sensitive teaching model and instruction design in the EFL teaching process as shown in Figure 1.1.

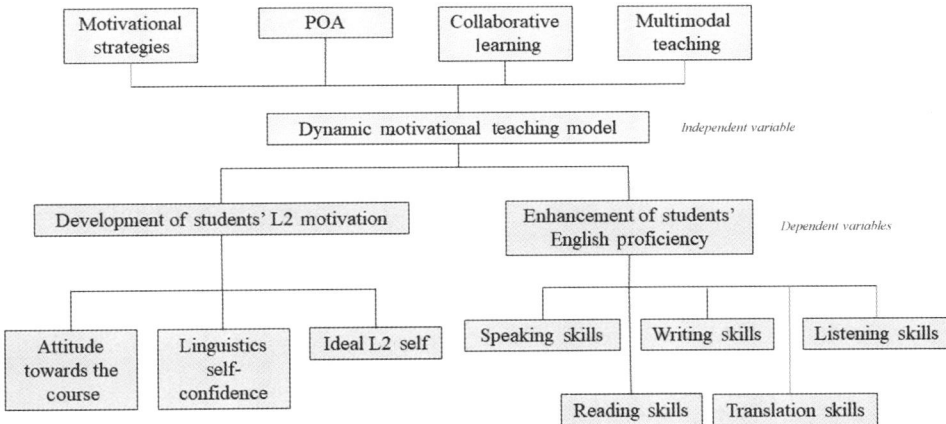

Figure 1.1 Conceptual Framework

1.6 Scope of the Study

This research was designed as an experimental study with an experimental group and a control group. The participants of this research were two natural parallel classes of non-English major freshmen in Anhui Polytechnic University. The experimental group was taught by the researcher and was treated with the dynamic motivational teaching model, while the instruction of the control group was implemented by another teacher, the researcher's colleague with over 10 years' teaching experience. Students in the control group were taught in the traditional way. The teaching experiment lasted for one semester, 14 weeks, with 3 hours for each week of the first semester in the academic year 2019–2020.

Both quantitative and qualitative methods were adopted to conduct this research. Qualitative research instruments were two times self-reports written by experimental students, one after the first unit teaching and the other toward the end of the semester during the process of the implementation of the dynamic motivational teaching approach. The quantitative study was carried out through students' L2 motivational questionnaire and students' English language proficiency in the experimental class and the control class before and after the implementation of the dynamic motivational teaching model in the experimental class. The English language proficiency tests included the oral test and the written test, the scoring of which was responsible by the researcher and the teacher of the control group.

1.7 Definitions of Terms

The terms defined in this section include (1) dynamic motivational teaching model, (2) English language proficiency, (3) experimental group and control group, (4) high/medium/low achievers, (5) L2 motivation, and (6) traditional teaching.

Dynamic Motivational Teaching Model: It refers to a combination of three crucial teaching components with motivation strategies into a dynamic framework, which can systematically function on the intensity of students' L2 motivation in a pleasant and stimulating setting.

English Language Proficiency: It refers to the ability to speak English, or to accomplish different language tasks in EFL. In this study, the five classical elements—speaking, writing, listening, reading and translation were used to measure the EFL learners' language proficiency.

Experimental Group and Control Group: In this study, the author chose two parallel non-English major natural classes from Anhui Polytechnic University for the experiment with one being the control group and the other the experimental group. While the experimental group was treated with the dynamic motivational teaching model by the researcher, the control group was instructed with the traditional method by another teacher with over 10 years' teaching experience. Except that, the two groups showed no evident differences in English language proficiency represented by college entrance examination and other factors such as age, gender and English learning experience.

High/Medium/Low Achievers: The participants were divided into three levels according to their scores in their English in the entrance examination. As the total score is 150, the high-achievers defined in this study are students who score over 120, the medium-achievers are the students whose scores are between 119 and 105, and the subjects with scores lower than 104 belong to the low-achievers.

L2 Motivation: With all the diversity of the definition of L2 motivation, this study adopted Dörnyei's definition as the research foundation which states that the role of motivation is to stimulate the L2 learners' original driving force and provide sustained power for the future learning process. Four dimensions were employed to examine learners' motivation state in this study: attitude towards the L2 course, linguistic self-confidence, ideal self-confidence and classroom anxiety.

Traditional Teaching: Under traditional teaching, or regular college English classroom, the standard teaching procedure is pre-reading, while-reading and after-reading. The instruction basically happens only in the classroom with the teacher lecturing and students listening and taking notes, and the materials mainly taking the textbook as the single resource for teaching and learning.

1.8 Significance of the Study

Due to the accelerating globalization and the fact that English has been developed an international language, China is in an urgent need of talents in good command of English to promote the communication and cooperation with people from other countries. However, despite a long period of English learning from the elementary schools to universities, most undergraduate students still cannot meet the social requirement of comprehensive application of English. Traditional teaching method has to share at least part of the blame for this situation. Because of this, this study tries to construct a motivation-centered instruction model for English class, design teaching procedures, implement experimenting teaching and to carry out a comprehensive study of the relationship between motivation-oriented instruction and the effectiveness of college English teaching. This research has some innovative significance and practical value in related theoretical exploration, research content, research method and so on.

First, this study integrates theory with practice and devotes to enrich and develop the depth and extension of a teaching mode. By absorbing the essence of the three teaching components—POA, collaborating learning, multimodal teaching, and the motivational teaching strategies, this research proposes a conceptual college English teaching model and designs an operational program diagram of motivational teaching model to give implications to college English teachers who also want to use alternative teaching methods to enhance students' motivation, and therefore, to achieve optimal teaching results.

The second is its theoretical and practical significance. Although based on output-driven and input enabling, the POA in English teaching has been confirmed of many benefits compared with traditional one, it is mainly on the theoretical level, and because it is not long since it came into being, there is a severe shortage of empirical research on the POA. The same situation can also be seen of motivational strategies. While there is a general belief that the teachers' use of motivational strategies can promote students' motivation, most studies have conducted research by surveying the teachers' perceptions of its importance and frequency of use (Cheng & Dörnyei, 2007; Dörnyei & Csizér, 1998), and few empirical evidences have confirmed teachers' use of motivational strategies and their motivational practices are the positively related with their students' motivation (Guilloteaux & Dörnyei, 2008). This study, by conducting a semester long research, tries to provide empirical evidences to the two theories.

Last but not least, there is significance on the subjective choice and content. To achieve an ideal learning outcome, what matters is not only how teachers teach but also how students learn. A key problem in foreign language teaching is how to stimulate students' learning potential since students' lethargy and non-achievement norms (or "norms of mediocrity") in the classroom are regularly reported to be basic hindrances to effective teaching (Kubanyiova, 2006). Thanks to the hard work of previous research on L2 motivation in context, we now have a package of motivational strategies available on hand. However, no matter how capable a teacher is of manipulating motivational strategies, it is unreasonable to anticipate that students' motivation will sustain long if the teacher still uses the long been criticized teaching method with no intention to make an innovation. Out of this consideration, this research embeds motivation theory and motivational strategies into three motivational variables in language teaching context, which can be seen as a dynamic system with the four variables interacting with one another, and language teaching and learning as a dynamic process, together promoting the learners' L2 acquisition by stimulating students' interest and internal motivation in language learning.

1.9 Organization of the Study

The book consists of five chapters: introduction, review of related literature, research methodology, research findings, and conclusion, discussion, and recommendation.

In the introductory chapter, research background and broad rationale behind the study are presented. This is followed by review of literature, which defines the concept of relevant theories and summarizes the research at home and abroad. It begins with the relevant research of L2 learning motivation and motivational strategies, then theoretical foundation and relevant study in China and around the world of three motivating teaching factors: POA, collaborative learning and multimodal teaching that are provided respectively. The final part of this section is contributed to a brief review on the development of research on the model of teaching. All of the five theories lay a foundation for the design of the dynamic motivational teaching model. Chapter 3 is the core part of the study, which includes the research design, followed by a description of study participants, sample and research instrument, then moves on to data collection and data analysis. The construction of the dynamic motivational teaching model is also illustrated in this chapter. Then Chapter 3 is brought into a conclusion with the data analysis. Chapter 4 reveals the results of the quantitative study on the impacts of the dynamic motivational teaching model on the EFL learners' motivation intensity and L2 language proficiency by comparisons of motivation and language proficiency improvement between the dynamic motivational teaching model classes and the traditional English classes. The effectiveness of this new teaching model is also tested through the qualitative study, i.e. students' self-reports. Chapter 5 is the final part. In this part, the major findings of the empirical research are summarized, and the problems and shortcomings of the research are pointed out, as well as the suggestions for future research.

Chapter 2 Review of Related Literature

This chapter defines the concept of the main theories in this study and summarizes their relevant researches in China and around the world. It begins with literature concerning L2 motivation from three aspects: the most influential L2 motivation theories/models, Motivational Teaching Practice (Dörnyei, 2001) and L2MSS (Dörnyei, 2005, 2009), and then moves on to the three important components in language instruction: POA, collaborative learning and multimodal teaching, each involving its concept, theoretical foundation and relevant empirical study. The final part of this section is devoted to a brief review of research on foreign language teaching models in China and abroad, revealing the main characteristics in different teaching models, which provides implications for the development of the dynamic motivation teaching model in this study.

2.1 Literature Review of Motivation

2.1.1 Definition of L2 Motivation

There is a clear agreement that L2 motivation plays a significant role in determining success or failure in L2 learning. Motivation is not only the catalyst of L2 learning but also the key to sustaining the drive to make the necessary effort, "without sufficient motivation, even individuals with the most remarkable abilities cannot accomplish long-term goals, and neither are appropriate curricula and good teaching enough on their own to ensure students' achievement" (Dörnyei, 2005). The last few decades have witnessed a considerable interest generated in L2 motivation among scholars and researchers. When it comes to the definition of motivation, however, little consensus has achieved due to the versatility and complexity that can influence human's behavior, just as Dörnyei said, "Motivation is one of the most elusive concepts in applied linguistics and indeed in educational psychology in general." Therefore, the studies of motivation are more often than not approached or selected from one particular aspect of motivation or another (a key concept or process). For example, Gardner (1985) believes that L2 learning motivation refers to the desire to achieve the goal of learning a language and the combination of efforts made and a good attitude towards learning the language. Brown (1994) states that L2 learning motivation is the choice of the goal and the degree of effort made to achieve it. From the perspective of social construction, Williams and Burden (1997) maintain that L2 learning motivation is a state of cognitive and emotional stimulation, which leads to a conscious decision of action and a sustained intellectual or physical effort to achieve one or more of the previously set goals. Addressing the process of motivational development over time, Dörnyei and Otto (1998) define motivation as "the dynamically changing cumulative arousal in a person that initiates, directs, coordinates, amplifies, terminates, and evaluates the cognitive and motor processes whereby initial wishes and desires are selected, prioritized, operationalized and (successfully or unsuccessfully) acted out". Different scholars have provided definitions that represent their own perspective and research orientation towards motivation, but no matter from which perspective is these theories put forward, two factors can be seen included in these expressions: L2 learning desire and efforts for L2 learning.

If learners have a strong desire for foreign language learning and make continuous efforts towards it, the enthusiasm of foreign language learning can be improved. Learning enthusiasm is the internal driving force of learning behavior, which has a direct bearing on the frequency of students' using L2 learning strategies and actively participation in learning activities, and the influence of learning motivation on learning results is realized by regulating learning enthusiasm (Xu & Feng, 2012). Therefore, a strong learning motivation of foreign language can affect learners' enthusiasm for foreign language learning, thus affecting its results.

2.1.2 Multi-Studies of L2 Learning Motivation

Motivation theory includes the use of human instinct, the need level, the use of internal drive and other modern psychological theories to explain motivation. The theory of second language motivation not only has the characteristics of the above general motivation theory, but also has its own linguistic characteristics. It is generally believed that the theoretical study of second language motivation has gone through three stages of development: the social psychology stage between the 1950s and the 1990s, the cognitive-situated period in the 1990s, and the process-oriented stage at the turn of century. In order to better show the internal logic and development of the second language motivation theory, the main theories are presented according to the time sequence, and each theory is explained in combination with its development and derivative logic.

2.1.3 Gardner's Integration Motivation Model

Working in the bilingual social context of Canada, Wallace Lambert and Robert Gardner aroused their interest in the study of second language motivation. They believed that second language was an important mediating factor between different language groups and served as the main force to promote or hinder cross-cultural communication. As early as 1959, they published a series of studies on the influence of learning attitude and motivation on L2 learning achievement, and pointed out in 1972 that cognitive factors and learning opportunities could not fully explain the personality differences of second language, suggesting that motivation played an important role.

The most important contribution of Gardner and his colleagues to the theory of second language motivation is the Socio-Educational models, involving four classes of variables: the social milieu, individual differences, language acquisition and contexts, and outcome (Gardner, 1985). It is emphasized that second language acquisition is carried out under a specific cultural background, which is an important prerequisite for understanding other factors. At that time, Gardner put forward three important elements of second language motivation theory: motivation intensity and efficiency, desire for language learning and attitude towards language learning. In his view, motivation is a very important spiritual "engine" or "mental engine" or "energy-center", which consists of three components: effort, cognition (want/ will), affect (task enjoyment). The two closely combine with each other to influence the effect of second language learning.

Besides, Gardner also put forward a very important concept of orientation in his theory of L2 motivation in 1985, when he stated that the theory of second language motivation was about the relationship between motivation and orientation with the later exerting a significant role in inducing the former, though it was not a part of motivation. On this basis, Gardner pointed out two types of orientation: instrumental and integrative. While the instrumental orientation is easier to understand, referring to the relatively utilitarian goals that drive language learning, such as better job opportunities or higher salaries. The integrative orientation represents the most elaborated and widely spread study of Gardner, which is defined as the willingness to be like valued members of the language community, and is a positive disposition to interact effectively with and becomes a member of a second language group (Gardner & Lambert, 1959). It includes three important aspects: integrativeness, including interest in foreign languages, and attitude towards second language, reflecting the willingness to interact with second language groups; attitudes towards learning situations, involving language teachers and second language courses; and motivation, comprising effort, desire and attitude towards learning. (See Figure 2.1)

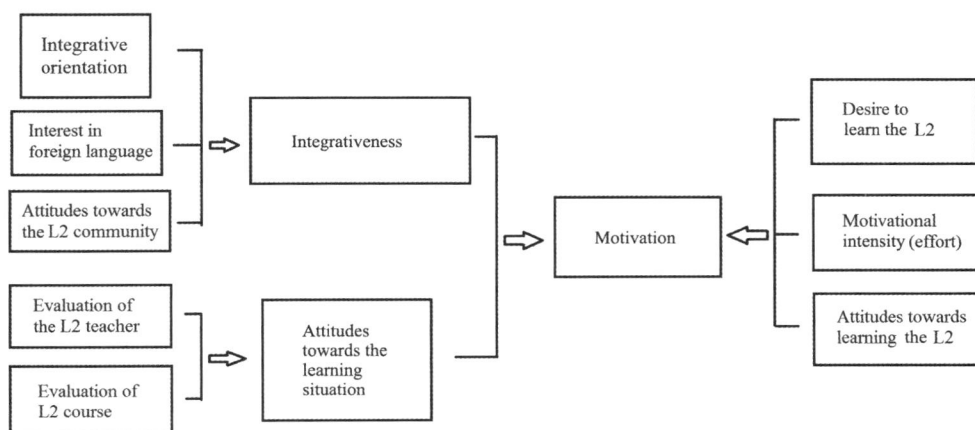

Figure 2.1   Gardner's Conceptualization of the Integrative Motive
Note: Cited from Dörnyei & Ushioda (2009).

The study of Gardner and his partners has opened up a new field of "social psychology" for the theory of second language motivation, and provided a pioneering exploration for subsequent researchers. According to Dörnyei, these theories are more valuable than previous studies. The concept of motivation, social education model, integration orientation and Attitude/ Motivation Test Battery (AMTB) put forward by Gardner have been widely used in the study of second language motivation. However, Gardner's social education model and the theory derived from it are not perfect without criticism. (Dörnyei, 1998; Dörnyei & Otto, 1998). It is found that while integrative orientation is an important means to stimulate second language motivation, the instrumental orientation can also not be ignored (Noels et al., 1999), Au posits that the integrative motivation concept "lacks generality" (Au, 1988). Some other criticisms focus on the lack of attention to the dynamic change of learning motivation in Gardner model, which sets second language learners as a stable and constant state, when learning motivation is actually a dynamic process (Dörnyei, 2001), and the model is not detailed and complete, at least not including the external factors of second language motivation (Dörnyei, 2005). In addition, under the condition of globalization, the model does not fit in with the current "global multilingual".

2.1.4 Tremblay and Gardner's Model of L2 Motivation

With the deepening of the study of L2 motivation theory, the social psychological model established by Gardner cannot meet the needs of scholars for the further exploration in the L2 motivation field, and it is urgent to introduce an alternative perspective to closely relate with motivation in specific learning context,more systematic and accurate theories to lead the research trend of second language motivation. Meanwhile, by constantly revising and supplementing the previous second language motivation theory, and in response to the "adoption of a wider vision of motivation" (Tremblay & Gardner, 1995), Tremblay and Gradner (1995) complete the extended motivation model (as shown in Figure 2.2). Combined with the expectancy-value theory and the goal theory of motivation psychology, the model inherits the structure of the linear relationship between language attitude, motivation behavior and academic achievement, and adds three mediating variables: goal salience, valence and self-efficacy. Thus, it can be seen that by absorbing a lot of knowledge of cognitive theory and adding some cognitive factors and situational factors related to classroom teaching, it is an innovative extended theoretical framework in what is called the cognitive-situated period by Dörnyei (2005).

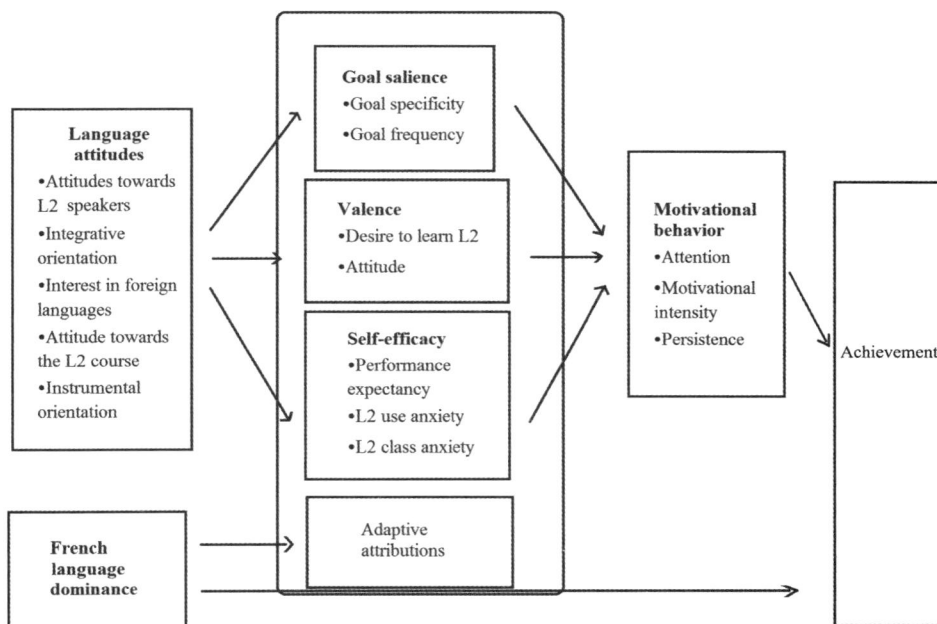

Figure 2.2 Tremblay and Gardner's (1995) Model of L2 Motivation
Note: Cited from Dörnyei & Ushioda (2005).

2.1.5 Williams and Burden's Social Constructivist Model

Although Tremblay and Gardner's extended motivation model has supplemented the factors related to second language teaching on the basis of the previous social-educational model, it cannot highlight the characteristics of classroom environment, and Williams and Burden (1997) develop a new motivation model based on social constructivism theory as shown in Figure 2.3. Because it pays attention to the motivation analysis related to second language learning in classroom environment, it is more meaningful for teachers engaged in second language teaching. The most important contribution of the model is to divide the second language motivation into two parts: internal and external factors. The internal factors include learners' age, gender, interest, attitude, initiative, learning desire, self-concept, emotional state and language development stage, while external factors comprise learning environment, interpersonal relationship (relationship with parents, teachers and classmates), etc. Internal and external factors are interrelated and influence each other in the process of motivating motivation. For example, the learner's self-efficacy and values may affect his learning attitude, and the learning environment may also affect the teacher-student relationship.

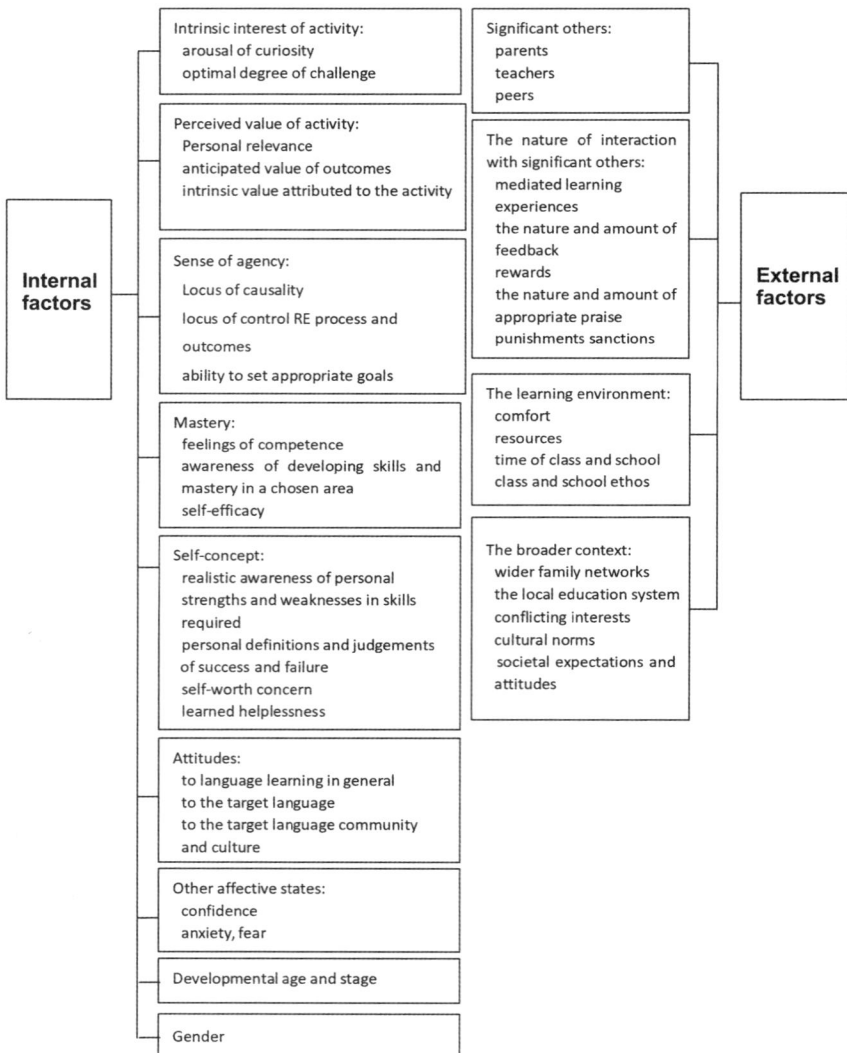

Figure 2.3 Williams and Burden's Framework of L2 Motivation

Note: Cited from Williams & Burden (1997).

2.1.6 Dörnyei's Three-Level Framework of L2 Motivation

In the 1990s, with the cognitive theory used by many scholars to carry out in-depth study of second language motivation, second language learners' beliefs about their abilities, potentials and limitations as well as the past language learning experience have been paid more attention than before (Dörnyei, 2005). Of course, the innovation of theoretical research is not out of thin air, and many theories are revised on the basis of their predecessors and the fusion of other subject theories, such as Dörnyei's three-level framework of motivation, which has become an important theoretical achievement.

The theory mainly defines and measures second language learning motivation from three different dimensions: language, learner and learning, in which the language level draws on and complements Gardner's integrative-instrumental dichotomous method, and analyses the social factors of second language learning motivation. The learner level mainly points to learners' sense of achievement and self-confidence. While self-confidence is related to learning ability, anxiety, attribution and self-efficacy, the achievement is the embodiment and result of learners' self-confidence, the two interacting with each other. The learning level focuses on the curriculum, teacher and learning team. Based on this, Dörnyei and Csizér (1998) by survey, extract the ten most effective macro strategies for language learning—the Ten Commandants. Because the three-level theory has combined language learning motivation with teaching scenarios, including some factors ignored by Gardner (such as the evaluation of cohesion within the learning group), it is of practical significance to teachers' classroom guidance. However, Dörnyei and Csizér (1998) criticize the lack of relationship between the components of language learning motivation in the motivational construction framework, and the "goal" elements described in the self-determination theory (Deci & Ryan, 1985) is not included in this motivational structure. This triggers a reconceptualization of motivation along with the missing nature of existing structural definition as described earlier.

2.1.7 Self-Determination Theory

At the end of the 20th century, with the continuous progress of the study of second language motivation, the focus on the concept of integrative motivation and society gradually became less and less, shifting to pay attention to the problems related to teaching practice, such as the influence of L2 learning situation on L2 learners' motivation. Self-determination theory became one of the important motivation theories in this period. As a more elaborate update theory from the traditionally well-known distinction in motivation theory: intrinsic versus extrinsic motivation, where the extrinsic motivation can be seen as something that can spoil intrinsic motivation, Deci and Ryan's self-determination theory views extrinsic motivation as a continuum representing different degrees of harmony between an individual's own way, and an externally prescribed way of thinking or behaving. That is to say, there is not necessarily a negative relationship between the two forms of motivation. Four types of extrinsic motivation are distinguished in self-determination theory which lays a cornerstone for this theory: external regulation, introjected regulation, identified regulation, and integrated regulation, with the latter two explained and analysed by instrumental motivation (Dörnyei, 1994).

On the basis of self-determination theory, Noels (2001) puts forward a relatively large motivation structure, consisting of three interrelated orientations: inherent reasons, external reasons and comprehensive reasons in the process of language learning, which is helpful in offering a theoretical framework for classifying and organising language learning goals or orientations in terms of a self-determination continuum. In addition, their situated classroom-focused research has highlighted features of the social learning setting which may influence the development of students' intrinsic or extrinsic motivation (Dörnyei & Ushioda, 2011).

2.1.8 Dörnyei and Otto's Process Model of L2 Motivation

Based on the advantages of previously existed motivation theories, and noticing their limitations of three aspects: lack of a comprehensive description of motivation influencing factors, paying more attention to the impact of motivation on behavior choice rather than behavior performance, and the neglect of the fluctuation of motivation of specific learners' behaviors or classroom processes over time, Dörnyei and Otto (1998) propose an L2 process model by synthesizing various lines of research on motivation in the L2 field and in educational psychology within a unified framework, which becomes the most developed and comprehensive theory to explain L2 motivation. This theory organizes a series of discrete behavioural events that initiate and implement motivational behaviour through two dimensions: action sequence and motivational influences, where the action sequence is a process that consists of the initial hope, the desire to commit to the goal, and then into the intention, leading to the final action until the goal is reached. Motivational influences, and the second dimension of the model, are the motivational forces in the course of behaviour.

Drawing on Heckhausen and Kuhl's (1985) action control theory, Dörnyei and Otto have divided the motivational behavior process into three main stages: pre-actional, actional, and post-actional. The pre-actional phase can be understood as the choice motivation leading to the target and task selection. It can be further categorized according to the order into goal setting, intention formation and the initiation of intention, and the motivational influence in this process is mainly reflected in: values-related L2 learning process, the achievement and the consequence, the attitude towards L2 and its speakers, the degree of expectation for success, the confidence and strategy of learning, the support and limitation of environment, etc. Actional phase is the process of motivation execution, which has three basic processes: decomposing the task into short-term goals and units, evaluating the process in the learning environment to monitor the progress of achieving the goal, and applying the action control mechanism or self-regulation strategy to enhance or maintain the motivation. The main motivational influences of this stage are reflected in learning experience, the social impact of teachers, parents, peers, classroom feedback and goal-building, self-regulation strategies and so on. The post-actional phase is a review after the behavior completes or is possibly interrupted for a period of time. Learners compare their initial expectations with actual results and then form causal attributions to guide their subsequent action plans. Attributional factors, self-concept beliefs and external feedback and achievement grades are the factors that affect the post-actional stage.

2.1.9 The L2 Motivational Self System

Advanced from Gardner's (1985) integrative and instrumental motivation concepts of the Socio Educational Model (SE), and integrated with psychological theories of the self, Dörnyei's (2005, 2009) L2MSS offers a new approach to understand language learning motivation, "a shift that reflects a general trend in mainstream motivational theories, but gains its decisive impetus from the specific link between language learning and notions of self and identity" (Vera, 2009). It is based on the theory of possible selves (Higgins, 1987; Markus & Nurius, 1986) and self-discrepancy theory (Higgins, 1987). The possible selves are visions of the self in a future state, representing the "individuals' ideas of what they might become, what they would like to become, and what they are afraid of becoming" (Markus & Nurius, 1986), and due to its future-oriented characteristic, i.e. it concerns one's hope and aspire, the possible selves can act as future self-guides towards behavior. The concept of possible selves has been later further developed by Tory Heggins (1987), who according to its guiding function to academic function, divides the possible self into two types, the learner's ideal self and ought self, with the ideal self referring to the "representation of the attributes that someone would ideally like to possess (i.e. a representation of hopes, aspirations, or wishes)" and the ought self being defined the "representation of the attributes that someone believes you should or ought to possess (i.e. a representation of someone's sense of your duty, obligations, or responsibilities)". Both kinds of selves have the function of guiding an individual's behavior by highlighting the discrepancies between the current actual and the future desired selves, which are followed by, according to the self-discrepancy theory, the action to reduce the gap.

Rooted on possible selves theory, especially learner's "ideal L2 self", plus the substantial impact of students' learning environment on students' motivation and learning achievement, Dörnyei (2001) constructs his L2MSS, which is composed of the following three components: the ideal L2 self, the ought-to L2 self, and the L2 learning experience. The ideal L2 self refers to the L2-specific facets of one's ideal self. It concerns the hopes, aspirations or wishes related to L2 that one would like possess, or the vision of oneself as an effective L2 speaker, therefore, it can play the role of powerful motivation, guiding the learner's academic behavior to narrow the gap between the current and ideal selves and achieve a high level of L2 proficiency. The ideal L2 self is related to the traditional integrative motivation and the internalized instrumental motive. The ought-to L2 self corresponds to Higgins' (1987) ought self, which refers to the duties, or responsibility that one believes one ought to have to meet the expectation of the social outsides in concerning the L2 and avoid possible negative outcomes as well. It is related to the less internalized type of traditional instrumental motive (Gardner, 1985). The L2 learning experience concerns the situation-specific motive connected to the immediate classroom learning situation or the past learning experiences, or elements such as curriculum, L2 teaching material, teacher and peer group. It is based on the finding that for some students, they are not initially motivated to learn another language due to an internally or externally generated self-image, but to their previous positive language learning experiences.

2.1.10 L2 Motivational Strategies

2.1.10.1 Motivational Teaching Practice in the L2 Classroom Framework

As the study of second language motivation in foreign countries has gradually changed from the orientation of social psychology to the orientation of school education, many researchers have diverted their attention to classroom teaching environment, exploring the factors that affect learning motivation, especially offering teachers significant practical implication to stimulate and maintain students' learning motivation in order to improve teaching quality and achieve teaching goals. For example, Brown (1994) believes that in order to stimulate students' inherent motivation, it is necessary for teachers to design knowledgeable teaching content and classroom activities, to develop learners' ability to learn independently, so the student-centered cooperative teaching should be promoted. Raffini (2010) believes that the indiscriminate use of material rewards and penalties will seriously weaken students' internal motivation. Therefore, more efforts are advocated to make for teachers to improve students' learning autonomy, to increase the sense of belonging, to enhance self-esteem, and to encourage students to participate in and enjoy the learning process. Lavin (2004) believes that teachers must strategically use internal and external motivation to promote students' learning. It is suggested that the teacher can improve students' internal motivation by arousing their interest, maintaining their curiosity, using a variety of interesting teaching methods and helping students set learning goals. They can also use some external incentives, such as clear expectations of students, timely and clear feedback and so on. However, Dörnyei and Ushioda (2011) argue that "while there are many effective motivational principles and guidelines that can help practitioners, these principles do not add up to a coherent theory". Instead, Dörnyei (2001) offers a comprehensive summary of motivational techniques based on the process-oriented model which in many ways more logical than making somewhat arbitrary decisions about which central themes the material should be built around, and these motivational strategies are presented via Motivational Teaching Practice in the L2 Classroom framework. "Following through the motivational process from the initial arousal of the motivation to the completion and evaluation of the motivated action" (Dörnyei & Otto, 1998), Dörnyei (2001) summarizes 35 specific classroom strategies which are further broken down into over 100 motivational techniques that can be used by teachers to promote L2 learning motivation under four major themes (as shown in Figure 2.4):

a) Creating the basic motivational conditions;

b) Generating initial motivation;

c) Maintaining and protecting motivation;

d) Encouraging positive retrospective self-evaluation.

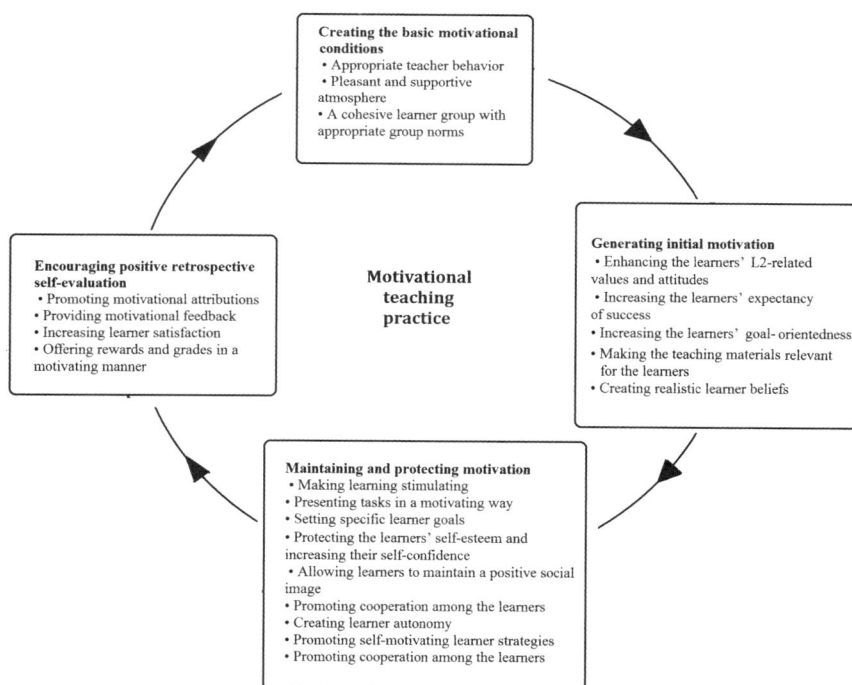

Figure 2.4 The Components of Motivational Teaching Practice in the L2 Classroom

Note: Cited from Dörnyei (2001).

2.1.10.2 Creating the Basic Motivational Conditions

Dörnyei (2001) argues that three preconditions must be satisfied before effective strategies to generate or maintain motivation can be adopted. The results of surveys (Chambers, 1999; Dörnyei & Csizér, 1998) indicate that the most important factor contributing to a student's positive or negative appraisal of L2 learning is the teacher, therefore, appropriate teacher' behaviors come as the first precondition to create the basic motivational condition. And this precondition consists of being enthusiastic about language learning, showing students that their learning matters, having high expectations, and building warm personal relationships with students and their parents. Based on the idea that the teacher's interest and passion towards the subject matter and his teaching can be infectious and ignite the same willingness for students to pursue knowledge, Dörnyei (2001) proposes the enthusiasm as an important ingredient of the appropriate teaching behavior, and the strategy in line with this is that the teacher should demonstrate and talk about his own enthusiasm for the course material, and how it affects his personality. Showing commitment to and expectation for students' academic progress is another factor contributing to students' motivation which can be achieved by offering concrete assistance, offering to meet students individually to explain things, responding immediately when help is requested, allowing students to call the teacher at home when they have a problem, etc. Besides, building good relationships with students and their parents are also included in the motivational teaching practice.

The second precondition is a "pleasant and supportive classroom atmosphere", referring to both the psychological and physical environment of the class to reduce the language anxiety created by a tense classroom climate which is found one of the most powerful factors hindering L2 learning achievement (MacIntyre, 2002; Dörnyei, 2001). This is not difficult to understand because the learners are under great pressure when they operate in a new language system with limit language knowledge, having to take considerable risks to produce the target language which involves pronunciation, intonation, grammar and content at the same time (Dörnyei, 2001). The strategies to create a motivating classroom environment involve building rapport with students, establishing norm of tolerance and using the technique of humour.

The third condition concerns developing a cohesive learner group with appropriate norms. To achieve this, Dörnyei suggests that it is necessary for the teacher: (1) to promote interaction, cooperation, sharing of personal information and group tasks and activities, (2) to use ice-breakers at the beginning of a course, (3) to establish group norms and have them discussed by the whole group. The reason why a cohesive learner group is so emphasized in regards to learner's motivation is that "group as a social unit exerts a powerful influence on its members' behaviours", "student motivation tends to increase in cohesive class" (Dörnyei, 2001). This is due to the fact that in a cohesive class, L2 learners share responsibility to achieve the L2-relavant group goals, and they support each other, thus feeling more comfortable in the positive relations while enjoying the learning process.

2.1.10.3 Generating Initial Motivation

As L2 learning is not selected based on students' interest and willingness, and most students find the classroom experience quite boring, it is suggested that the teacher should contribute to generating positive attitude towards their learning. Enhancing learners' language-related values and attitudes is on the top of the strategies to achieve this goal which can be divided into three types: the intrinsic value, intercultural value and instrumental value, each corresponding to learners' genuine interest in L2 learning, L2-related culture and the practical benefits that might be associated with the mastery of the L2. It is suggested that these language-related values can be enhanced by exposure to respected peer models who can be invited to class to share their positive experience, providing to students the views of their peers and by associating students with peers who are enthusiastic about L2. As for how to arouse the learners' intrinsic interest in L2 learning, highlighting the positive aspect and organizing some enjoyable L2 activities are considered useful. Additionally, an increased learners' expectancy of success also plays a significant role in increasing students' desire to learn which can be promoted by providing students with sufficient preparation and assistance and helping to remove potential obstacle to success. Furthermore, due to the important role of goal in directing students' performance and inspiring effort, an enhanced learners' goal-orientedness can also contribute to students' willingness to learn and the teacher can facilitate this by negotiating and formulating a common goal. After that, it is important to make sure that the tasks and activities for the students are those that serve the pursuit and attainment of the goal. The fourth aspect of generating initial motivation is making the course materials relevant to the learners. It needs little justification for this because students will not be motivated to become learners unless they regard the material they are taught as worth learning (Dörnyei, 2001). This factor can be achieved by relating the subjects to everyday experiences and backgrounds of the students, and there are two steps that are suggested to follow: the first is to use the analysis of students' needs to identify their interests, hobbies and needs of learners, and then to link classroom topics and activities to the students' real-life experiences and preferences. The last factor Dörnyei (2001) proposes for the initial motivation is to create realistic learners' beliefs which include how difficult it is to learn L2 language, how fast one can expect to make progress, what is required to be successful as well as how language is best learned. Because unrealistic learners' beliefs can be detrimental to the mastery of L2 learning, it is suggested that the teacher should make students aware of the non-easy process of learning L2, and different learning methods and strategies that suit students themselves best should also be encouraged for them to explore (Dörnyei, 2001).

2.1.10.4 Maintaining and Protecting Motivation

Since the nature of motivation is dynamic, which is vulnerable to fluctuate due to a diversity of motivational influence during the long and difficult L2 learning process, it is unreasonable to expect the motivation maintain all the long. So it arises an important question "How to ensure the continuity of learners' motivation?". In response to this, several countermeasures are offered in Dörnyei's (2001) motivational teaching practice. The monotony of the classroom flow can be broken by adding variety to the language tasks, teaching process and the general rhythm and sequence of contents, and this can contribute to making learning stimulating and enjoyable, which can be collaboratively achieved by making the tasks intriguing, encouraging more involvement and presenting tasks in a motivating way. Besides, as opposed to the class general goal mentioned in the second stage, setting a specific and measurable, challenging and realistic goal can go a long way to help the learners to structure the learning process. Furthermore, in order for the students' focus on learning with vigour and determination, rather than giving up easily because of self-considered aptitude deficiency, it is the teacher's responsibility to enhance the learners' self-esteem, positive social image, and learner autonomy. To achieve this goal, other techniques such as reducing language anxiety, teaching learner strategies, promoting cooperation instead of excessive use of competition among students are also proved to be helpful for students' motivation. Another dimension worth highlighting is promoting self-motivating learner strategies. It is true that university life is so rich and colourful that it is replete with diverse distractions. There are so many places and so much time that is beyond the teacher's control. To succeed academically, "students must learn to cope with the competition between their social and intellectual goals and to manage and control the range of other distractions that arise" (Corno, 1994). Therefore, whether or not learners manage to master the skills to deal with negative factors hindering their academic achievement, self plays a significant role in the maintenance and protection of motivation. To achieve this, the teacher can share with students the self-motivating strategies divided by Dörnyei (2001) into five main classes: commitment control strategies, metacognitive control strategies, satiation control strategies, emotion control strategies and environmental control strategies.

2.1.10.5 Encouraging Positive Self-Evaluation

Here the self-evaluation refers to the learners' appraisal of and reactions to their own past performance. Because how the students interpret their past failure or achievement will exert a big effect on their future L2-related experiences, teachers should play a big part in helping learners to consider their past performance in the following constructive ways: (1) attributing their past failure to little work or insufficient knowledge instead of lack of ability or aptitude; (2) providing motivational feedback about the progress the learners are making and about the areas which they still need improvement; (3) increasing learner satisfaction by taking time to celebrate any big or small victory and involving task which allow students to public display their projects or skills; (4) offering rewards and grades in a motivating way, for example, offering rewards for participating in activities and providing grades that can also reflect effort and improvement.

Although displaying a rich variety of useful motivational strategies and techniques, Dörnyei does not think a little that all of these strategies should be applied to be a motivation-sensitive teacher, instead, it is a conscious choice and implementation process based on the learners' cognitive learning methods and approaches, thus, he advocates quality rather than quantity. That is to say, a teacher should only choose some strategies which he thinks to suit him and his learners to be a motivating teacher and to create an overall positive motivational climate in the classroom.

2.1.10.6 Empirical Validation of Motivational Strategies

Although L2 motivation researchers generally believe that the application of motivation teaching strategies can improve learning motivation, there is a lack of empirical data to support this theoretical hypothesis (Bernaus & Gardner, 2008). Therefore, by means of questionnaire, Dörnyei and Csizér (1998) investigate 200 Hungarian English teachers on the importance they have attached to these motivational strategies and the frequency they actually have employed them in their practical teaching. They sum up the "Ten Commandments on Motivating Language Learners" which can effectively stimulate students' learning motivation, that is, (1) to set a personal example with your own behaviour; (2) to create a pleasant, relaxed atmosphere in the classroom; (3) to present the tasks properly; (4) to develop a good relationship with the learners; (5) to increase the learner's linguistic self-confidence; (6) to make the language classes interesting; (7) to promote learner autonomy; (8) to personalize the learning process; (9) to increase the learners' goal-orientedness; and (10) to familiarize learners with the target language culture. To test the situational applicability of these macro strategies, Cheng & Dörnyei (2007) repeat Dörnyei & Csizer's (1998) questionnaire, involving 387 English teachers from China where the culture background and educational context are quite different from that in Western countries. The study shows that most of the motivational strategies are consistent between the two studies, which demonstrates they are transferable across different teaching setting, such as "displaying motivating teaching behaviour", "enhancing learners' confidence in language learning", "creating a relaxed and pleasant classroom environment" and "presenting task appropriately". Some motivational classroom practices are indeed subject to cultural-specific constraint, such as "promoting learner autonomy", which is distinct from the situation in Hungary and rarely used by Chinese teachers. It is also found that compared to their Hungarian counterparts, the motivation strategy of "encouraging students to attribute success or failure to hard work" is especially valued and used frequently by English teachers in China. To further verify the relationship between motivation strategies and learning motivation, Guilloteaux & Dörnyei (2008), based on the framework of motivation strategies of Dörnyei (2001), use MOLT (Motivation Orientation in Language Teaching) scale to observe 40 English classes in the Korean foreign language teaching environment. The frequency of use of motivation strategies and classroom motivation behaviours are recorded, and then 1,300 students' English learning motivation are investigated. The results show that the use of motivation strategies is helpful to improve students' English learning motivation and classroom involvement. In addition to investigating the practical effects of motivation teaching strategies in the language classroom, their research for the first time uses empirical data to prove the relationship between motivation teaching strategies and learning motivation. Bernaus and Gardner (2008) also investigate 31 Spanish English teachers and 694 students in order to explore language teaching strategies and the effects of these strategies on students' motivation and proficiency. This study indicates that teachers and students do not agree on the frequent use of all strategies and it is the students' perceptions of these strategies, rather than teachers' reported use of motivational strategies that has a positive effect on students' English proficiency, attitude and motivation. In other words, the effective teaching must be based on the students' perceptions of the teaching strategies.

Many of the studies in this field in China also focus on the frequency of teachers using strategies in classroom and the effect of these strategies on students, for example, Ji (2004) uses the questionnaire to investigate the awareness and use of motivation strategies in college English teachers and finds that motivation strategies which teachers consider important are not often used in their practical teaching. Zhao and Wang (2002) carry out a survey of 103 high school teachers in three cities of Shandong Province to measure their awareness of the importance of motivation strategies and the frequency of the use of motivation strategies. The main finding is that the teachers agree on the importance of motivational strategies in classroom and actively practice strategies such as setting a good example, establishing a good teacher-student relationship, enhancing students' self-confidence in language learning, creating a pleasant classroom environment, encouraging students to attribute success or failure to learning, etc., but some strategies which are related to group activities and games are ignored and less used, and diversification of classroom activities and learning tasks as well as the selection of task within students' reach are also inadequately used. You (2010) carries out a quantitative study on English teachers' motivation teaching strategies in senior high schools and finds that there are significant differences between urban and rural high school English teachers in the use of classroom motivation teaching strategies.

Motivation strategies have attracted certain attention from researchers in China. Most studies employ questionnaires and interviews as research tools to explore a set of teaching strategies that can effectively stimulate students' motivation, and few empirically examine the exact relationship between teachers' motivational strategies and students' motivated learning behaviors. However, Xu and Feng (2012) employ questionnaire, classroom observation and interview to explore the internal relationship between the application of the motivation strategy and the students' learning motivation and their classroom motivational behavior. The results show that the use of teacher classroom motivational strategies not only directly affects students' immediate response in class, but also has significant links to students' overall motivation tendency of the course.

2.1.11 Generating and Sustaining a Vision for Language Learning

Since we know the ideal L2 language plays a role in behaviour self-guides, how should we do to help students to develop an attractive ideal language self? Here, Dörnyei (2001) introduces an important component of L2MSS, the learners' vision of themselves in a future state, and asserts the central function of images and imagination in stimulating the motivation to learn through promoting a more vivid and elaborate mental representation of future self in the students. The introduction of the concept of vision makes the "possible self" in the theory of second language motivation self-system more visible and concrete. Motivation strategies to improve the ideal self are also designed around the establishment and development of learners' vision.

The following are the six components of strategic implications put forward by Dörnyei aiming to contribute to promoting students' motivation through vision which then leads to their valuable idea L2 self.

• Creating the language learners' vision. The concrete way is to raise the students' awareness about their long-cherished aspiration, dreams, etc., to arouse their attention of the importance of picturing a future ideal self-image.

• Strengthening the vision through imagery enhancement. This involves helping learners to build a vision as elaborate and vivid as possible, otherwise, a blurred and unclear vision cannot be expected to act as an effective motivator to energize the students' effort to reach it.

• Substantiating the learners' vision by making it plausible. This requires realistic expectations about their future ideal selves, avoiding self-deception, as well as considering any obstacles and difficulties getting in the way of achieving the ideal self.

• Developing an action plan. In order to transform the vision into action, a package of suitable plans including at least a goal and study plan are indispensable to channel the energy into constructive routes towards success.

• Keeping the vision alive by activating the ideal L2 self. The specific approach is to use effective tasks and activities, and engaging students in target language related culture such as music and film to regularly remind students of their ideal self.

• Counterbalancing the vision by considering failure. In other words, envisioning a feared self that the failure would lead to in order to obtain a maximum effectiveness of the vision, involves reminding students of the negative consequences of not succeeding as well as the duties and obligation imposed from the learners' ought-to L2 self.

L2MSS provides a direct theoretical support for the study of L2 motivation strategies (Yang & Li, 2010) and the last few years have seen more and more scholars combine their research with L2MSS, with a large number of studies conducted to examine and validate this theory in different countries where English is used as a foreign language. For example, Japanese scholar Sampson (2012) conducts a corresponding action study on the lack of motivation in Japanese college English classes. Based on the six components of L2MSS, and his study formulates corresponding motivation strategies and it is found that the motivation strategy aimed at improving the "ideal second language self" of learners effectively improves their second language motivation. Similarly, Magid (2014) also confirms that by enhancing the ideal second language self of fifth graders in Singapore, they can improve their learning motivation and self-confidence. One study based on L2MSS worth mentioning is conducted by Magid and Chen (2012) who use two novel intervention programs to enhance participants' visualization of their ideal L2 selves. Both programs have lasted from three to four months in two different countries, China and England. By designing activities which involve listing goals, drawing a timeline, developing action plans and considering feared selves, and introducing the Ideal Self Tree activity, both programmes are effective in motivating the participants to learn English and increasing their linguistic self-confidence through strengthening their vision of their ideal L2 selves. Inspired by Magid and Chen's programme, Zeynep Erdil and her colleague (2016) develop a speaking task by asking the participants to send message to themselves from their future self. The results also prove a positive impact on the participants by demonstrating a higher motivation after one semester's treatment.

Numerous studies show that L2MSS is a powerful framework to examine and explain the complex L2 motivation construct and the ideal L2 self a valid and reliable construct explaining a noticeable portion of variance in learners' intended effort (Csizér & Kormos, 2009; Papi, 2010; Ryan, 2009; Taguchi et al., 2009; Thompson & Erdil-Moody, 2014). However, as to the ought-to L2 self, there is not much empirical support for the ought-to L2 self as a valid construct, but Csizér & Dörnyei (2005) and Kormos & Csizér (2008) find the less overall impact of the ought-to L2 Self on learners' motivated behaviour compared to the ideal L2 self. A survey carried out by Papi (2010) on a number of 1,011 Iranian high school students finds that while the ideal L2 self and the L2 learning experience decrease students' English anxiety, the ought-to L2 self significantly makes them more anxious. L2MSS also enjoys a certain amount of attention of many Chinese scholars. Wang and Dai (2015) conduct a 14-week study on motivation strategies of 111 non-English major freshmen. The results show that learners generally consider these strategies to be effective and their ideal L2 selves are significantly improved, but further investigation shows that learners' motivation status has not been significantly improved. Ge and Jin (2016) study 196 universities freshmen in non-English major to explore the relationship between L2MSS and English learning effectiveness, and find out that there are differences in the self-system of L2 motivation between boys and girls, with the level of L2 motivation of girls generally higher than that of boys, and that there is a positive correlation between L2 motivation ideal self-level and English achievement.

It is based on Dörnyei's L2 motivational strategies framework as well as the theoretical framework of L2MSS that this research establishes its motivation-sensitive teaching practice in the English teaching process.

2.2 The Production-Oriented Approach

The POA is proposed by Chinese foreign language educators, represented by professor Wen Qiufang (2015, 2016). With the attempt to overcome the weakness of traditional Chinese English teaching, it is an innovative teaching theory integrating the strengths of Western instructional approaches and Chinese contextual features. The development of the POA theory has undergone three phases: the earliest version was output-driven hypothesis (Wen, 2008) based on the study that output is more powerful than input in motivating for students to learn a foreign language; then, it was developed to the output-driven and input-enabling hypothesis with the emphasis on the role of input in enabling learners to perform better in the output; and finally the POA as a whole was brought into being in October, 2014. Over the past years, this method has inspired a great enthusiasm among those innovative college English teachers and scholars and has been widely applied in English classroom teaching with fruitful results yielded.

2.2.1 Theoretical System of the POA

There consists of three components in the theoretical system of the POA: teaching principles, teaching hypothesis, and teaching procedure. While teaching principles serve as the theoretical guidance of the other two parts, teaching hypothesis functions as the theoretical support of teaching procedure, and teaching procedure is the realization of teaching concept and hypothesis, with the intermediary role of teachers reflected in each link of the teaching procedure. Figure 2.5 shows the theoretical system of the POA and its relationship.

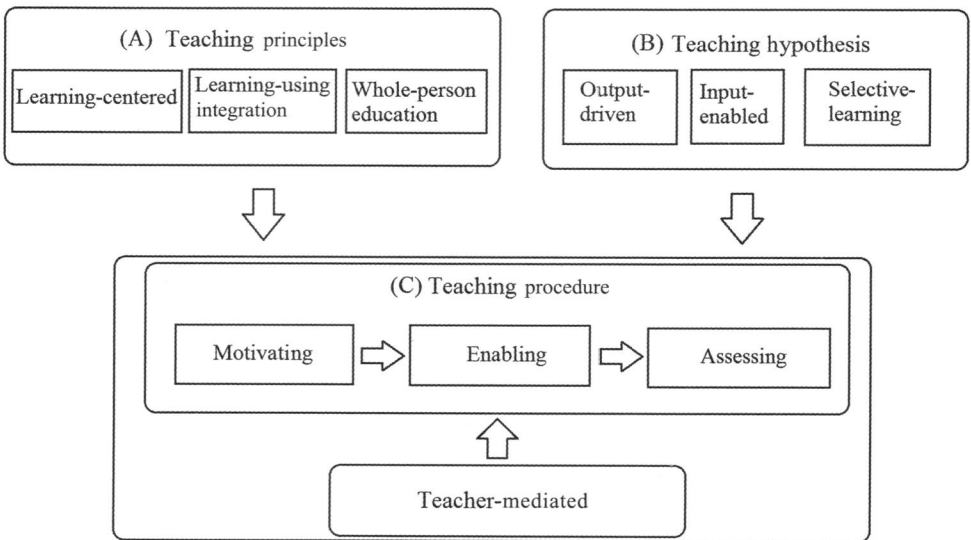

Figure 2.5 Theoretical System of Production-Oriented Approach
Note: Cited from Wen (2016).

2.2.1.1 Teaching Principles

The teaching principles compose of "learning-centered principle", "learning-using integration principle" and "whole-person education principle".

"Learning-centered principle" advocates that all activities of classroom teaching should "serve the effective learning" (Wen, 2015). It not only opposes the "teacher-centered theory" where the teacher alone has the say or what implements is cramming education, but also opposes "students-centered theory" under which the students' activeness, interest and experience are too much emphasized and the teacher's professional function is downplayed.

In "learning-using integration principle", "learning" means input, and "using" means output. The integration of learning and using advocates that to learn is to use, and learning and using at the same time. This principle not only opposes the current teaching mode of "text-centered" in Chinese universities, but also opposes task-based teaching method and project teaching method which characterize the excessive emphasis on the use of language while ignoring the language learning under the teachers' guidance.

The "whole-person education principle" starts from the viewpoint that English language teaching should not only be satisfied with cultivating students' second language communicative competence, but also serve to foster the college students' humanistic qualities, such as cross-cultural communicative competence, autonomous learning skills and critical thinking abilities, etc., to produce socially developed and globally aware citizens (Wen, 2015).

2.2.1.2 Teaching Hypothesis

The teaching hypothesis is the theoretical support of the teaching procedure, including the "output-driven hypothesis", "input-enabling hypothesis", "selective-learning hypothesis" and "promoting learning through assessment hypothesis".

The "output-driven hypothesis" draws inspiration from Swain's (1985, 1995) Output Hypothesis and Long's (1996) Interactive Hypothesis (Gass & Mackey, 2006). It argues that language learning with output can achieve better learning results than language learning without output (Wen, 2016). Output is both the driving force and the goal of language learning.

The "input-enabling hypothesis" assumes that while learners can activate their stored knowledge, and enhance language fluency in the process of completing the task, the teachers should provide students with appropriate materials or explanation, in order to promote students' comprehension input, expand their knowledge system, and to improve the quality of students' output.

"Selective-learning hypothesis" proposes that selective learning optimizes learning effects better than non-selective learning. "Selective-learning" means "selecting useful parts from the input material as required by the output activity". This hypothesis opposes the indiscriminate teaching as displayed in the traditional teaching model, and the "output-oriented method" uses language learning materials as facilitating material rather than learning objectives, and advocates the selection of parts beneficial to output activities in the limited class time, while ignoring the irrelevant parts.

"Promoting learning through assessment hypothesis" means that students should assess their written production under the guidance of teacher while learning instead of after learning, and should regard assessment as the strengthening and deepening stage of learning instead of two separate things.

2.2.1.3 Teaching Procedure

The teaching procedure of the POA consists of three phases: motivating, enabling and assessment. In each stage, teachers should play the mediating roles which include guiding, designing, and scaffolding (Wen, 2016).

2.2.1.4 Motivating

Different from other teaching approaches, and also a distinctive characteristic, the POA places motivating at the initial phase as shown in Table 2.1. The purpose of this is to make students aware of the inadequacy of their language knowledge in their attempts at the communicative activity, thereby creating a desire for the further learning.

Table 2.1 Tasks and Requirements of the First Motivating Phase

Tasks	Requirements
The teacher describes relevant communicative scenarios.	Scenarios with a high communicative value are required; and the topics for communication need to be sufficiency cognitively challenging.
Students try out the required productive activity.	Make students aware of their problems in accomplishing the required productive activities and arouse their desire for learning to overcome these deficiencies.
The teacher explains learning objectives and productive activities.	Enable students to recognize both communicative and linguistic objectives, and describe types of tasks and specific requirements.

Note: Cited from Wen (2016).

Table 2.1 illustrates the specific tasks with requirements during the first phase of instruction. First of all, the teacher should motivate students' interests by presenting a communicative scenario which they may encounter in their future studies and work, and also with certain cognitive challenge. Secondly, the students try to complete the production task so that the students can feel in their own experience that it is not easy to accomplish these tasks, thus giving birth to the motivation of the students to learn. Thirdly, the teacher illustrates what students are expected to achieve at the end of the unit.

Three standards have been pointed out to evaluate the effectiveness of motivating (Wen, 2017), and they are cognitive challenge, communicative authenticity and objective appropriateness, and for the objective appropriateness, the POA emphasizes obtainable communicative and linguistic objectives, which means the designed learning objectives necessarily vary according to students' diverse English levels.

2.2.1.5 Enabling

While the process of motivating is the innovative part of POA, the stage of enabling proves the most crucial one during which the teacher provides selective input materials and guides students in learning step-by-step to complete the assigned productive task. Table 2.2 presents the specific tasks and requirements of the enabling phase.

Table 2.2 Tasks and Requirements of the Enabling Phase

Tasks	Requirements
The teacher explains how the productive tasks are to be accomplished, the enabling materials to be given or to be searched, and what learning objectives are to be achieved.	Familiarize students with the tasks, procedures, and specific requirements for each step.
The teacher divides a large productive task into several mini-tasks and provides students with the enabling materials accordingly.	Make sure students are able to describe the logical links between these mini-tasks and the links between segments of given materials and each mini-task.
Students read or listen to the given materials selectively while the teacher gives guidance and checks their learning outcomes.	Enable students to select relevant ideas, language, and/or discourse structures from the given materials.
Students practice a mini-productive task once they finish their selective learning of the given materials.	Prompt students to use what they have just learned from the given materials to accomplish their productive task.

Note: Cited from Wen (2016).

As to what should be chosen to learn from the selected materials and how to choose the enabling teaching materials from the bewildering amount of information available in the modern society thanks especially to the rapid development of the Internet, Wen (2017) discusses that relevant ideas, language expressions and discourse structures should be the priority for the assigned productive activity. And she emphasizes that only the input material which directly serves as the means and tool to complete the production should be selected and processed. Besides, three criteria are proposed to evaluate the effectiveness of the enabling activities: precision, progressiveness and diversity.

2.2.1.6 Assessing

Under the guidance of the idea that assessing is an extension of assessment, and the purpose of assessment is to help students learn further. The POA attaches great importance to assessment which can be divided into two categories: formative classroom assessment and achievement assessment. The former refers to the instant assessment taking place in the enabling phase when students make selective learning and practice the sub-tasks, and the later refers to the delayed assessment which waits until students finish the learning of related knowledge and extracurricular practice before they submit their output production to the teacher for evaluation. The POA takes the achievement as its focus. Table 2.3 presents the tasks and the requirements of achievement assessment.

Table 2.3 Tasks and Requirements of the Assessing Phase

Tasks	Requirements
The teacher and students set up criteria of assessment together.	Make criteria clear, comprehensible and easy to check by students themselves.
Students submit their products to the teacher.	Submit the product with an acceptable format before the deadline.
The teacher and students evaluate the typical products collaboratively in class.	The teacher prepares before class to ensure that evaluation comments are to the point and relate to students' production, and enables all students to participate in assessment by all means.
The teacher and students evaluate the remaining products after class.	Put each student's personal products with assessments in portfolios as part of the grade for this course.

Note: Cited from Wen (2016).

Integrating and absorbing the advantages of various evaluation methods, Wen (2016) creates teacher-student collaborative assessment (TSCA), which is also a characteristic and innovation of the POA. In this type of assessment, the teacher chooses the evaluation focus and the typical sample, reads over and remarks before the class, then the students in the class carry on the evaluation with various types of organization, according to the evaluation focus under the guidance of the teacher. It is worth noting that the criteria for assessing are whether the production objectives as well as the quality of the product are achieved instead of considering the quality the only target.

2.2.2 Relevant Studies on the POA in China and Around the World

A large number of research and teaching experiments have been conducted on the POA to test the feasibility and effectiveness of the POA on foreign language teaching. For example, in the related research of writing teaching, Qiu (2017), through the experimental teaching of a unit, discusses the effect of the POA on college English writing. The research shows that the POA teaching of a unit has little influence on the overall quality of the student's writing, but compared with the traditional teaching method, the students of the POA teaching class have a better grasp of the unit target language, with more use of these language items in the composition. Zuo (2018) combines the POA with the thinking map and carries out the teaching of college English writing for a period of one month. It is found that this teaching model plays an active role in the overall writing improvement of the students in the experimental group, because in this way, the students can really apply what they learn to use which in turn promotes their learning through the using. Li (2017) conducts a comparative study on the oral output ability of the POA and PPP (Presentation, Practice and Production) teaching. The result shows that the POA teaching method is more effective than PPP in improving the oral English performance of non-English majors. In the aspect of oral output, the POA teaching method is more effective than PPP teaching method in fluency and complexity, but there is no difference in accuracy, and the reasons need to be further studied and explained.

In addition to the study of the validity of oral and writing English, the POA has also been proved the vitality and effectiveness in interpretation (Jiang & Meng, 2017) and phonetic teaching (Cao, 2017) as well as in the humanistic quality education (Qi, 2016) to improve the students' thinking ability and classroom efficiency. What is worth mentioning is the study of Zhang (2017), who conducts a semester's teaching experiment to test the overall teaching effect of the POA, which makes up for such shortcoming of previous researches as limited students' change observed and learning effect due to the short duration. It is found that there is no significant difference in the overall English level between the experimental group and the control group, but the listening and writing levels of the experimental group are significantly improved and they also show very positive attitude towards the POA and their motivation to learn English is obviously strengthened.

While a large number of studies are devoted to proving the effectiveness of the POA in English second language classroom, some researchers turn their attention to a more micro level—how to effectively implement a certain link in the POA teaching. For example, by describing the whole process of micro-course production and its repeated modification in detail, Yang (2015) reports how to design micro-courses to realize the motivating link of a certain unit. Based on the teaching practice of language enabling. Qiu (2017) explores the preliminary principles for effective language promotion in the enabling phase. Sun (2017) applies the teacher-student collaborative assessment of the POA in classroom reflective teaching for one semester and explores the operational principle, means and effect of "Teacher-Student Cooperation Evaluation". Cao (2017) puts forward two dimensions of teacher scaffolding based on the POA framework: vertical scaffolding and horizontal scaffolding, and illustrates how to build teacher scaffolding in providing guidance and assistance in terms of content, language and discourse.

Despite the fact that the POA is becoming more and more popular in China, as a completely new teaching theory system, it also poses great challenges to teachers who wish to take advantage of this innovative teaching approach (Zhang, 2017). First, distinct both from the traditional "text centre" which is a one-way knowledge teaching mode, and from the imported teaching model of "student centre" where the teacher assigns tasks to students and asks them to construct the knowledge by themselves, the "learning centre" advocated by the POA may make the novice teachers feel confused in their initial attempt. Moreover, the appropriate and good use of the principles of the POA, i.e. "Motivating", "Enabling", and "Assessing", are very challenging. Second, in order to give full play to the teaching effect of the POA, there is an urgent need to have a curriculum system to support the theory, including the teaching material and the evaluation system, etc. Without the evaluation system closely matched to it, some students are worried about the English final term exam or other proficiency tests in the process of their POA English learning (Zhang, 2017). Still another challenge may come from the non-English major students who, under the background of the exam-oriented learning setting, have the L2 learning motivation, learning attitude and learning strategies running encounter to the requirement and purpose of the POA. Therefore, it is crucial for teachers to have a good command of the theory and flexibly use the theory according to the specific teaching situation, in order to deal with various challenges and achieve a better teaching effect.

2.3 Collaborative Learning

2.3.1 Characteristics of Collaborative Learning

To collaborate is to work with another or others. Collaborative learning (CL) means students working in pairs or small groups to achieve shared learning goals. Slavin (1995) defines CL as a kind of class technique that "encourages students to perform all kinds of learning activities in group or small team, helps them study some materials and rewards students for achievements or performance of the entire group, enhances teacher-student, and student-student interactions, promotes students to carry out a cooperative learning efficiently". Johnson & Johnson (1999) see CL as "to work together to maximize the learning effects between themselves and others and achieve common learning".

To employ such technique successfully, three features should be made clear: (1) Carefully designed activities by teachers; (2) co-labouring, which means all participants in the group must engage actively in working together toward the same objectives; (3) meaningful learning must take place that can increase students' knowledge or deepen their understanding of course curriculum. Although there is another term for this kind of activity, cooperative learning, which has a similar meaning and is often used interchangeably, and this book uses collaborative learning rather than cooperative learning because collaborative learning is appropriate for higher education while cooperative learning is used in children education (Bruffee, 1995). But besides that, there are other differences between cooperative learning and collaborative learning which are illustrated in the following Table 2.4.

Table 2.4 Differences Between Cooperative Learning and Collaborative Learning

Type	Essence of definition	Goals	Nature of knowledge	Role of teacher
Cooperative learning	The instructional use of small groups can make students work together to maximize their own and each other's learning. (Smith et al., 2005)	To work together in harmony and mutual support to find the solution	There is a "correct" answer or at least a "best solution", and that different students will have knowledge about different aspects of the task.	Subject matter expert and authority in classroom
Collaborative learning	Occurs when students and faculty work together to create knowledge. It is a pedagogy that has at its center the assumption that people make meaning together and that the process enriches and enlarges them.	To develop autonomous, articulate, thinking people	Knowledge is socially produced by consensus among knowledgeable peers. It is something that people construct by talking together and reaching agreement.	A member of a community in search of knowledge with students

But since some researchers are used to adopt the term cooperative learning in any educational level unselectively, we use the research results coming from the literature of both cooperative and collaborative learning.

2.3.2 Essential Elements for Collaborative Learning

At present, there are a great variety of cooperative/collaborative learning methods or strategies used in practice. Johnson brothers (Johnson D.W. & Johnson R.T., 1999) believe that for any successful cooperative learning groups, there are five elements that are considered indispensable.

(1) Positive interdependence. The success of individuals is linked to

the success of the group. Thus, the students should know that they must not only hold responsible for their own study but also should help other peers in their group in order to achieve the group goals. "It is not enough to simply tell students to work together; they must have a reason to take one another's achievement seriously." (Slavin, 1995)

(2) Promotive interaction. Students are expected to communicate face to face to offer an effective assistance and support to one another; to share learning resources; to provide their teammates with referenced feedback and to encourage each other's efforts to learn so as to promote one another's learning in their group.

(3) Individual accountability. Every student is required to be in charge of his own or his teammate's learning and contribute his share of work. There should be no "hitchhiking" or "freeloading" in the group. To achieve this, the teacher can give and assess each student's test or performance individually, observe the group discussion and record each member's contribution to his group work.

(4) Development of teamwork skills. Students are required to learn the interpersonal and small group skills for a high quality cooperation since researches show that the more socially proficiently students are, the higher accomplishment they are expected to achieve (Johnson D.W. & Johnson R.T., 1999). The basic social skills that students should be equipped with are as follows: a) to understand and trust each other; b) to express their ideas accurately; c) to help and support mutually; d) to try to resolve conflicts and contradictions constructively.

(5) Group processing. The group should regularly evaluate their collective activities, and review their group performance and productivity. By reflecting what member actions are facilitating or not, they can make decisions about what to strengthen or change.

2.3.3 Collaborative Learning Techniques

There are many cooperative learning techniques available to help teachers organize and conduct teaching in and after class, among which, techniques such as Learning Together, Jigsaw Grouping, Teams-Games-Tournaments, Group Investigation, Student Teams Achievement Division, Team Accelerated Instruction and Three-Step Interview (Kagan, 1994) are the most well-developed and easy to adopt. Methods employed in this study would be discussed in the following section.

2.3.3.1 Three-Step Interview

Three-Step Interview could be used as an icebreaker for group members to get to know one another better by asking probing questions and listening attentively. In this technique, students first interview each other in pairs, they then change their role as interviewers and interviewees, and finally they share the information they have learned from their partners with another pair in their group.

2.3.3.2 Think-Pair-Share

In this technique, students are first encouraged to think silently about the questions raised by the teacher. They may write down their thoughts, or just brainstorm them. Learners are then asked to work with their partners in pair, discussing his thoughts, and then listening to his partner. After pairing conversations, the teacher would solicit responses from the entire group.

2.3.3.3 Jigsaw Grouping

There are two versions of Jigsaw Grouping. In the original one, students are divided into two groups: home group and expert group. Students are assigned a different topic in the home group, and then they leave the home group and group with the other students with the same topic. They learn the material together, and then return to their home group and are responsible for teaching his assigned topic as an expert. In the later developed variation

(Slavin, 1995), members of the home group are assigned the same material but are accountable for different parts of the materials; each member must become an "expert" on his assigned section and then teach other members of the home group. In this study, the teaching activity is mainly based on the second one with adaption, because instead of teaching his other group member, the "expert" is required to teach the whole class.

2.3.3.4 Student Teams Achievement Division

Students are first presented with a lesson, and then they take a test on what they have learned. Although students are tested individually, they are graded on the team's performance, so they are encouraged to work together to improve the overall performance of the group.

2.3.4 Previous Study on Collaborative Learning in China and Abroad

Since rising in the United States in the 1970s, collaborative learning has gradually become the major means of teaching reform in various countries. The last few decades have seen extensive teaching practices and research conducted on collaborative learning and substantial progress made in their teaching theory and strategic system. Many studies have shown that collaborative learning is more effective at improving academic performance, promoting positive relationships, and higher self-esteem than competitive or independent learning (Johnson & Johnson, 1999; Liu, 2010). Johnson D.W. and Johnson R.T. (1999) find out that collaborative learning enables the group members have a higher level of thinking ability and a longer memory of the information. Gillies & Ashman (2000) also show that collaborative learning in English teaching creates numerous opportunities for students to interact, communicate, and support with one another, thus reducing learning anxiety and promoting the development of learners' English learning ability. Bölükba, Keskin and Polat (2011) propose that collaborative learning helps students to effectively participate in reading and learning and can create a rich, harmonious and healthy English learning environment, so as to make language learning more meaningful and promote language acquisition.

China began to study in group cooperation in the late 1980s, but it was until after the launch of the national basic education curriculum reform in the mid-1990s that collaborative learning was really valued and certain progress was made. Many domestic scholars have discussed the value of collaborative learning and its application in theory and practice. Zheng (2004) points out that the language environment is more real in the group collaborative learning process, so it provides many real listening and listening opportunities for college English learners. In this way, not only the classroom atmosphere is relaxed and lively, students' independent learning ability, interpersonal communication ability can also be developed. Kyndt et al., (2013) show that using group collaborative learning in college English teaching, students' achievement motivation level and their tendency to pursue success are significantly improved. Wu and He (2014) claim that collaborative learning can not only enhance students' writing motivation and writing interest, but also can help students to reduce writing anxiety and overcome writing difficulties to a certain extent, so as to further improve students' language application ability and writing strategy. The results of Li (2007) show that collaborative learning is suitable for large-class English teaching, which can improve students' English performance, especially oral English ability.

To sum up, the research on group collaborative learning in China and abroad has started early, and great progress has been made in the theory and application of group collaborative learning and has yielded many valuable research results. However, some studies have also shown that based on role division, reward and competition, collaborative learning is a reform of traditional teaching, due to the influence of cultural factors, it has also encountered difficulties to implement. Besides, if teachers' guidance is not well designed and their control are not effective, it is easy to subject from being a mere formality and the degree of students participation will not be high.

2.4 Multimodality and Multimodal Teaching

With the rapid development of multimedia technology, the communication mode, which used to be dominated by language and characters, has been gradually broken. Instead, various media technologies have been deployed to receive and transmit language, images, sound and other modes through visual, auditory, tactile and other senses. Different modes and media can coexist and interact with each other in the communicative process.

To understand modality better, it is necessary to make a distinction between "mode", "medium" and "modality". According to Kress (2003), mode refers to "a socially and culturally shaped resource for making meaning. Image, writing, layout, speech, moving image are examples of modes, all used in learning resources", while medium is "the substance in and through which meaning is instantiated/realized and through which meaning becomes available to others". Kress and van Leeuween (2001) conclude that multimodality is the use of several semiotic patterns to enhance or to complement or to hierarchically rank the expression of the same meaning in several relevant semiotic modes. Zhang (2009) also says that multimodality refers to the use of auditory, visual, tactile and other senses, through language, images, sounds, movements and other kinds of means and symbolic resources to communicate. Gu (2007) believes that there are three meanings for "multiple" in multimodality, it not only includes multiple channels of perception (e.g. auditory, visual, tactile, etc.), but also the material and technical media needed for communication, as well as various symbol resources such as language, images, sounds and movements which are produced through these channels and media. To make it simple, "modality" refers to the interaction between the human senses and the external environment, and multimodality means the interaction with more than three senses.

Multimodal teaching is to conceive the classroom into multimodal semiotic space. In the teaching of language, the meaning making modality includes linguistic, visual, auditory, gestural, spatial, and comprehensive use of the five models. Linguistic model is the main model of classroom learning, however, the role of non-verbal models in meaning representation and communication in teaching is becoming more and more important. For example, the teacher explains through the speech, while the image, gesture and other non-verbal models have the characteristic of intuitive expression, which can make a visual conclusion of the teaching content. Meaning is not expressed solely through language. Just as Hodge and Kress (1988) point out, meaning is not expressed solely through language, it also relies on the entire symbol system, which is a multimodal ensemble composed of models such as vision, behaviour, hearing, and language. In the analysis frame of multimodal semiotic, language is no longer a carrier of all meanings, but only a part of a multimodal ensemble, and models other than language can also realize communication and representation; various models of a multimodal ensemble have different communicative functions, and communicators achieve meaning making through modal selection and modal layout.

The theory of multimodal teaching emphasizes the development of learners' multiliteracies, and advocates an integrated use of graphics, video, audio to mobilize students as many senses as possible to enable students to feel the existence of the actual context. It can give learners a multi-sensory experience, and stimulate the enthusiasm and interest of students to participate in learning, communication, and class activities (Zeng, 2007). In the process of multimodal teaching design, thanks to the rich and diverse choices provided by multimedia and multimodality, teachers sort out and organize various materials to use in class in order to enhance students' interest in learning, and to create an autonomous learning environment for students to promote their knowledge comprehension and construction. By video, audio and other multimodal means, teachers offer a lively language environment for students to immerse themselves in them, feeling the cultural implication behind the language, thus obtaining the ability to use language.

2.4.1 Previous Research on "Multimodality Teaching" in China and Aboard

In 1996, the New London Group consisting of Bill Cope, Norman Fairclough, Jim Gee and Gunther Kress and other well-known scholars published *A Pedagogy of Multiliteracies: Designing Social Futures* and first proposed the concept of multimodality teaching.

In the field of education, multimodality analysis is generally combined with curriculum design and multimodality in teaching process, focusing on analysing the role of non-linguistic model and language model role in classroom teaching and design of teaching materials, as well as the effect of various models and media on teaching. For example, Guichon and McLornan (2008) study the effect of multimodality on L2 learners. They conduct experiments on Canadian non-English majors, which show that multimodality helps students understand listening materials better. O' Halloran (2004) explores diverse semiotic features of a mathematical text. Lemke (2002) points out that students in science classes should be equipped with multiliteracy to integrate and comprehend information transmitted by discourse, visual, and mathematical symbols, etc. Unsworth (2001) analyses the influence of multimodality expression system on curriculum design and implementation, and promotes multiliteracy teaching in primary and secondary schools. Royce (2007) attaches importance to the cultivation of students' multimodal communicative competence, and studies the complementarity of different symbols and the coordination of multimodality in second language classroom teaching. Kress (2003) develops a multimodal literacy theory framework, more comprehensively elaborated the multiliteracy ability, and discusses the media and modal evolution in teaching field, and the common features of modality and so on.

The concept of multiliteracy teaching proposed by the New London Group has received more and more attention in China, and has greatly influenced the content and methods of college English teaching. Related research have begun with Li's (2003) introduction of multimodal semiotics theory, who emphasizes its significance to English teaching. Hu (2007) introduces multimodal semiotics and multimedia semiotics, and thinks that the cultivation of multiliteracies should be given due importance. Gu (2007) constructs a model for analysing multimedia learning and multimodal learning. Zhu (2007) makes a comprehensive introduction to the initiative and content of the study of multiliteracy. Zhang (2009) establishes a comprehensive research framework of multimodality discourse analysis, and discusses the role of modern multimedia technology in foreign language teaching under this framework. Hu and Zhang (2013) present the results of a pilot study that the multimodal combination in teaching can mobilize the learners' sensory system to participate in learning. The multiple channel information can stimulate learners more intensely than a single channel of information, thus more conducive to the processing and memory of information, and finally can produce a good learning effect.

It can be seen that the application of multimedia in college English teaching makes the classroom more diversified and multimodality teaching meet the requirements of making foreign language teaching more vivid and interesting (Liu & Hu, 2010). Multimodal foreign language teaching has become an important part in the reform of foreign language teaching which can make up for the shortcoming of traditional single mode teaching method to a great extent. Therefore, this research intends to employ the theory of multimodal semiotics to construct the motivational teaching model for college English class in order to stimulate students' integration learning motivation to the greatest extent and improve the teaching effect of English.

2.5 The Literature Review of Teaching Model

2.5.1 Definition of Teaching Model

Although the concept of teaching model has existed for a long time, the fact that teaching model has really become an independent category in educational research is generally believed to begin with the research of Joyce and Will et al., (2004) who define the model of teaching as the creation of learning environment with long-range and short-term effects on students: "Content, skills, instructional roles, social relations, types of activities, physical facilities and their use all add up to an environmental system whose parts interact with one another to constrain the behaviour of all participants.... Different combinations of these elements create different environments eliciting different educational outcomes." According to them, a teaching model does not only provide information about how to design curriculum or plan lessons, but also help teachers while developing any kinds of instructional materials. Senemoğlu (2002) defines models of teaching as explanations for important variables which affect learning levels and their relationships in order to ensure learning as being the most effective and efficient. While Kilbane and Milman (2014) define models of teaching from the perspective of facilitating learning: "They are designed to promote specific learning outcomes related to required standards in the academic disciplines through the use of a specially set of activities." (Kilbane & Milman, 2014) From their perspectives, when a specific model of teaching is used, learners follow a sequence of steps to achieve learning outcomes in cognitive, affective and psychomotor domains. When developing a curriculum or planning a course, a teacher might use various models of teaching and design his/her instruction accordingly with the help of compatible instructional strategies, methods, techniques, and tactics.

The research on the model of teaching in China began in the 1980s, and the understanding of it can be roughly divided into the following categories from different perspectives: Firstly, it can be defined from the perspective of teaching methods, such as "the teaching mode is a dynamic system formed by teachers in the process of coordinated application of various teaching methods at different teaching stages according to the teaching purpose and teaching task" (Li, 2004). Secondly, it can be defined from the angle of teaching structure, for example, the teaching model is "the model of the structure of the teaching activity which reflects the specific teaching thought formed in practice", "the subjective choice of the teaching objective structure made by people under the guidance of certain teaching thought", and "the stable form of the teaching structure in the degree of space and time" (Hao & Xu, 2003). The third category defines the model of teaching from the viewpoint of design and organization teaching, as in "the model of teaching is formed according to the teaching thought and the teaching law, and it is the relatively stable teaching procedure and the method strategy system that must follow in the teaching process" (Zhen, 1984).

Therefore, it can be summarized that the model of teaching belongs to the category of teaching methods and teaching strategies, but not equal to them. Teaching method or strategy generally refer to a single method or strategy used in teaching, while teaching mode refers to a stable combination of two or more teaching methods or strategies. In the process of teaching, in order to achieve a certain expected effect or goal, it is often necessary to use a variety of different methods and strategies synthetically. When the combined application of these teaching methods and strategies can always achieve the expected effect or goal, they would become an effective teaching model.

In this study, the teaching model is defined as a systematic integration of various teaching strategies, method, teaching organization form and teaching means, which are expressed in the form of a brief language, a symbol or a graph, in order to create an ideal learning environment under the guidance of certain teaching theory.

2.5.2 The Study of Foreign Language Teaching Model

It has been a long history for the research on teaching mode in Western countries. Traditionally, there was a 5E (Engagement, Exploration, Explanation, Elaboration and Evaluation) teaching model. Gradually it was expanded to the 7E (Excite, Explore, Explain, Expand, Extend, Exchange, Evaluate) teaching model developed by Eisenkraft (2003). Based on the process of students learning inner activities, a nine-event teaching model was put forward by American educational psychologist Gagné (1977), attracting a large range of attention and sparking a wide range of empirical researches. Gagné's nine-events teaching model involves gaining attention, informing learners of the objective, stimulating recall of prerequisite learning, presenting the stimulus material, providing learning guidance, eliciting the performance, providing feedback about performance correctness, assessing the performance, and enhancing retention and transfer. Then, teaching model has further witnessed its development into a 5T which integrates online and school-based curriculum in the information environment, then Action Research Instructional Model) (Alcione et al., 2009; Woo, 2016), Design/ Creativity Loops Model (Clinton & B. Hokanson, 2012) and the ADDIE teaching mode proposed by Rabaa (2016), which are Analysis, Design, Development, Implementation and Evaluation.

The study of teaching model in China began in the 1980s, absorbing the current theories and experiences of foreign teaching modelling, and combining the actual situation of Chinese students in learning English. In recent years, the research hotspots of teaching model have been those revolved around students' autonomy, the teaching model based on content, and the blended teaching model.

The model of teaching centred round students' autonomous learning highlights the cultivation of the students' autonomous ability. Duan (2004) puts forward that currently the teaching model with teachers as the centre still exists, and must be transformed into the one with the students as the standard, talk as the way and the inquiry as the characteristics. Based on the modern learning theory of quality-oriented education, Hu (2005) points out the significance of constructing the teaching model of the autonomous inquiry learning in the network environment, and establishing the evaluation standard to compare the two basic models of the independent inquiry learning. Zhong (2006) points out that the key to the reform of the teaching model is the sustainable development of the self-ability of the students. Chen (2010) also claims that after the integration of computer, network and foreign language education teaching has made the teaching model change radically, the traditional teacher-centered theory has been broken, and it is of great importance to highlight the student-centered teaching method.

The content-based teaching model was first introduced into foreign language teaching by Cai (2012) who points out that the content-based teaching model takes the language as the medium of content learning, while the content as the source of language learning, with the two organically combined and promoting each other. Cao (2012) maintains that the content-based teaching model is more beneficial to cultivate students' emotion in English learning, enrich the use of effective learning skills and to promote the English comprehensive application ability, but there are also many problems in the specific application process, which need to be constantly improved in practice. Zhang (2016) believes that the content-based teaching model is the essential change of the traditional teaching model, and is the one which organically combines the subject knowledge content with the language acquisition goal.

Under the background of innovative development of Internet information technology and network media, nowadays, the classroom teaching of college English is striving to break the traditional teaching model, and reflecting the comprehensive application of offline flipped classroom and online MOOC autonomous learning. This breaks the limitations of traditional English teaching in time, space and resources, and maximizes the optimal allocation of English teaching resources and the cultivation of students' independent learning ability. Zhang (2011) builds a hybrid English listening and speaking teaching model supported by mobile technology. This model achieves the blending from five dimensions, which is the mixture of formal learning and extracurricular informal learning, teaching and autonomous learning, teacher leading and student subjectivity, traditional media and new media in the learning process, and English language knowledge and English listening and speaking skills in the learning process. Yang (2019) builds a SPOC-based university English teaching model and makes an empirical and comparative study on the effectiveness of the model. The results show that the blended teaching model can significantly improve students' comprehensive English ability. Duan (2020) conducts a motivation intervention experiment in a mixed teaching model, and the results show that blending teaching plays a significant role in improving students' L2 learning efforts, and has an effect on enhancing their foreign language learning motivation.

2.6 The Summary of Literature Review

Based on what have been reviewed, we can see that few teaching models focuses on stimulating students' L2 motivation, and the reason may be that the motivation for foreign language learning is a complicated research topic, with many other factors related to motivation and complex relationships between them (Meng, 2010). Thus, applying the motivational strategies in its contextual teaching factors to create an optimal learning environment has never been seen. The motivation is rich and intricate, and it may be unrealistic to expect a certain factor play a definite role in activating and maintaining motivation in a long run, to maximize the likelihood of beneficial students' L2 learning taking place, and a combined effort to make the positive interplay of different variables in the process of teaching happen can be a promising way out of solving the problem. Thus, this study proposes an integrated teaching model that incorporates a multitude of motivational variables in language teaching to deal with the rich, multiconstruct, and contextualized motivational system. In this model, the teaching contextual factors, that is, teaching method (POA), teaching organization (collaborative learning) and teaching means (multimodal teaching) cooperate and interact with motivational strategies, all impact learners' L2 learning motivation.

Chapter 3 **Research Methodology**

This chapter presents the construction and the empirical study of the dynamic motivational teaching model. It mainly comprises of three parts. In the first section, research design, research setting and sample as well as research instruments and procedures are described. In the second one, a conceptual framework of the teaching model is formulated and the characteristics of the dynamic motivational teaching model are provided, then follows a detailed account of how to implement this model of teaching in the practical teaching. Finally, instruments, procedures of data collection and data analysis are explained.

Motivation plays an important role in the L2 learning process, so the lack of which may lead to the language learning failure. This research aims to construct a motivation-oriented teaching model in college English classroom in order to stimulate students to learn, then an experimental study has been carried out to examine the effectiveness of this teaching model in increasing students' foreign language learning motivation as well as their foreign language proficiency. The followings are the research questions of this book.

Q1. What are the effects of the dynamic motivational English teaching model on the learners' motivation toward learning English as a foreign language?

Q2. What are the effects of the dynamic motivational English teaching model on the improvement of the EFL learners' language proficiency?

Q3. What are the effects of the dynamic motivational English teaching model on the high/medium/low achievers in a heterogeneous class?

3.1 Research Design

This research adopted both qualitative and quantitative method to examine the effectiveness of this newly developed teaching model. The independent variable is the dynamic motivational teaching model, and the dependent variables are students' English learning motivation and interest, as well as speaking and written academic achievements of students with different levels of English proficiency. The present study used a mixed method research, and an embedded experimental design (Creswell, 2015). The quantitative data was collected through the 6-scale motivation questionnaire and the scores of English proficiency test, while students' self-reports provided the qualitative data. The quasi-experimental procedure for both groups was administered in the following sequence. First, students were designated to be the experimental group and the control group, and each group was divided into three levels: high, medium and low based on their English scores in the entrance examination. Both groups of students were given the motivation questionnaire at the beginning of the course, and the English proficiency test was also administered to them as the pre-test. Then, a fourteen-week teaching experiment was conducted by the researcher adopting the dynamic motivational teaching model for the experimental group and the traditional teaching method by another teacher for the control group. Finally, after the instruction of 14 weeks, students' L2 motivation was measured repeatedly and their English proficiency was also examined as the post-test. The research designed can be represented as in Table 3.1.

Table 3.1 A Glimpse of the Research Design

Subjects	Research process			
Experimental group	Quantitative 1 ● Pre-motivation questionnaire ● Pre-English test	Intervention (14 weeks of teaching experiment of the dynamic motivational teaching model) Qualitative 1 ●Self-report	Quantitative 2 ●Post-motivation questionnaire Post-tests ●Self-report	Results (quantitative/ qualitative)
Control group	Quantitative 1 ● Pre-motivation questionnaire ● Pre-English test	Traditional teaching model	Quantitative 2 ●Post-motivation questionnaire ●Post-English tests	Results (quantitative/ qualitative)

3.2 Population and Sample

The population of the study included the first year students at Anhui Polytechnic University in China. The participants in both the experimental group and the control group were the first-year non-English major students. Once the researcher received the teaching task from the department secretary, she asked the permission from the dean of Foreign Language School where the researcher was employed in this university. After the request approval, the researcher had this class to be taught as the experimental group which were made up of three non-English majors: Human Resources, Textile and Garment, and Advertising. The students were grouped together through the university course online selective system. Then, to avoid any unfairness to students, and for the sake of research reliability, the researcher found another parallel class with students of the same major combination taught by another teacher with more than 10 years' teaching experience as the control class. By doing this, it could be ensured that the treatment group and control group showed no obvious differences in their English language proficiency and other factors prior to the experimental teaching program. There were 72 students in the experimental group and 70 in the control group. All students were offered the same course of College English 1, with the same designated course book New College English Integrated Course. The experimental group was treated with the dynamic motivational teaching model, while the control group was taught with the regular teaching method commonly practiced in China. Apart from that, the other things such as teaching curriculum, teaching course book and the learning environment were the same. The basic lesson plan for the control group included a warming up activity to activate learners' background knowledge, skimming and scanning to obtain the main idea as well as the specific information of a text, explanation of the key and difficult language structures, words and expressions, and then a variety of exercises following the text that included reading comprehension questions and fill-in-the-blanks or translation aiming to strengthen the understanding and usage of the language items (See Appendix H for a model teaching plan). Both groups were given 14 weeks of instruction with 4 periods and about 3 hours per week.

As is introduced above, there were 72 students in the experimental group and 70 in the control group, while all the subjects were measured on their motivation twice at the beginning and end of the semester, only 42 students from each group participated in the oral and written test. The reason was that the length of the oral test for each examinee was 11–14 minutes. To ensure the secrecy of the test questions, that is, the content of the test was not disclosed, all the candidates needed to be tested at the same certain period. Considering the large size of the class, and the long duration for each examinee, the number of participants had to downsize. The selection of the sample in the oral and written test was as follows: First, students in both the experimental group and the control group were divided into three subgroups according to the English score of their entrance examination. The freshmen of both groups whose total scores fell into the scope of the top 30% of the total population were considered the high achievers. The students who scored within the bottom 30% of the whole population in this group belonged to the low achievers and the participants whose scores were between the two groups constituted the medium achievers. Then, 14 students from each level of proficiency: high, medium and low were randomly selected, together constituting 42 subjects in both the experimental group and the control group.

3.3 Research Instrument

In this study, a variety of data sources were collected using a range of research instruments for triangulation, so as to avoid the bias springing from a single viewpoint and to achieve a better understanding of the effects of motivational teaching model. Both qualitative and quantitative methods were used to collect data through the adapted motivational questionnaire, and students' self-reports.

3.3.1 Student Motivational State Questionnaire

The Student Motivational State Questionnaire adopted in this study was a combination from Erdil (2016) with some adaptation. The purpose of this questionnaire is to assess the students' situation-specific motivational disposition toward the English course before and after the experiment. The questionnaire was divided into four sections—attitudes toward the course, linguistic self-confidence, ideal L2 self and L2 classroom anxiety—totalling 26 questions, with each of the questions ranking 1 (strongly disagree), 2 (disagree), 3 (somewhat disagree), 4 (somewhat agree), 5 (agree) and 6 (strongly agree) on Likert scale (See Appendix A). A 6-point Likert scale was employed because by doing so, students were less likely to play safe and choose the middle number like 3 in the 5-point Likert scale, thus the validity of the questionnaire could be guaranteed. The items were first translated from

English into Chinese by an expert to avoid the confusion or misunderstanding that might be caused by difficult English words or structures. All of the participants were required to complete this motivational state questionnaire before the experimental teaching began and the same questionnaires were given to the students in both groups again when the experiment ended. To avoid the confusion or any other disturbance presented by foreign language, students were monitored during the whole process.

The questionnaire was piloted in October 2019 at Anhui Polytechnic University with a sample student group (N=35) of non-English majors. Before the piloting, it was validated by three experts, and some adaptations were made, for example, "as negative statement leading to reverse calculation, items with negative statements should have been grouped together under the classroom anxiety to be able to calculate in the same direction". After the piloting, the coefficient score at 0.939 indicated that the items in the questionnaire were at a high level of reliability and that the items in the questionnaire were closely related to each other. Table 3.2 shows the reliability coefficient for individual sections.

Table 3.2 Reliability of the Questionnaire

Items	Number	Cronbach's Alpha
Overall	26	0.940
F1 (Attitudes Toward the Course)	5	0.779
F2 (Linguistic Self-Confidence)	7	0.848
F3 (Ideal L2 Self)	6	0.880
F4 (L2 Classroom-Use Anxiety)	8	0.858

In order to effectively examine the intensity of the L2 Learning motivation, an exploratory factor analysis was also conducted on the 26-item scale to see if the questionnaire (as shown in Table 3.3) has a meaningful factor structure and if each item could correspond to the main factor of the L2 learning motivation.

Table 3.3 KMO (Kaiser-Meyer-Olkin) and Bartlett's Test of
Motivational Questionnaire

Items	KMO	Bartlett's test of sphericity		
		Approx. ChiSquare	*DF*	*Sig.*
Total	0.848	1065.207	325	0.000
Factor 1 (9)	0.789	93.490	10	0.000
Factor 2 (8)	0.840	169.736	21	0.000
Factor 3 (6)	0.843	186.835	15	0.000
Factor 4 (8)	0.813	232.909	28	0.000

As seen in Table 3.3, the KMO measure is 0.848, to be specific, except for Factor 2 (0.789), all other three factors are above 0.8, higher than the acceptable cut-off points of the KMO index which should be no less than 0.5, and the Bartlett's test correlation matrix is 0.000. This suggests that the correlation matrix is not an identity matrix. Therefore, the sample is fit for the factor analysis and the scale is valid in the sense of the construct.

3.3.2 Tests

With the purpose of evaluating the effectiveness of the dynamic motivational teaching model in enhancing language learners' English competence, CET-4 written test and IELTS oral test were given to all participants before and after the teaching experiment. CET-4, the abbreviation for College English Test Band 4, is a national large-scale standard English test conducted by the Ministry of Education. The purpose of the examination is to "accurately measure the comprehensive application ability of English of college students in China, in order to play a positive role in achieving the teaching goals of college English course" (Su, 2019). The CET-4 written test is divided into objective questions and subjective questions. Objective questions include listening comprehension and reading comprehension, which make up for 70% of the total score of the test paper; subjective questions include translation and writing, accounting for 30% of the total score of the test paper. Because the objective question has a fixed and single answer, from the perspective of scoring, it can basically ensure the objectivity and consistency of the test results, and has a very high test reliability, however, it is difficult to ensure a high test validity (Wu, 2007). At the same time, with no fixed and single answer to the subjective questions, translation and writing can directly detect the students' language application ability, therefore validity of the test is high (Su, 2019). With the questionnaire, the written test was also piloted and Cronbach's alpha reliability coefficient obtaining at 0.917 indicated that the items in the test were related to each other.

To measure participants' competence in the use of spoken English, the International English Language Testing System (IELTS) was adopted to test the students' oral proficiency. The test uses a nine-band scale to clearly identify levels of proficiency, from non-user (band score 1) to expert (band score 9). There are three parts to the test: interview, individual long turn and two-way discussion, and each part fulfils a specific function in terms of interaction pattern, task input and test takers output respectively. The grading of the communicative competence is based upon four criteria: (1) fluency and coherence; (2) lexical Resource; (3) grammatical range and accuracy; (4) pronunciation.

The same oral and written task were administered twice in the beginning of the semester as the pre-test and the second one toward the end of the semester as the post-test to figure out if there was any difference before and after the treatment in terms of the participants' English speaking and written level of performance.

3.3.3 Self-Report

To provide insightful information on students' learning experience of the dynamic motivational teaching model, students' self-reports are an important source, including their overall feeling over this dynamic motivational teaching model, their gains, difficulties and suggestions, which can be used to hear different voices from the participants about the effects of teaching model and prepare for future improvement. In this study, students were required to submit two self-reports during the process of the whole semester, one was after the complete of the first unit, and the other when the whole teaching experiment finished. Requirements of permission were asked from the students for all the data collected from them for the study.

3.4 Developing a Dynamic Motivational Teaching Model

As discussed before, a teaching model is a systematic integration of various teaching strategies, method, teaching organization form and teaching means in order to create an ideal learning environment under the guidance of certain teaching theory. Given the complexity and multidimensional nature of L2 learning motivation, this motivational teaching model proposes to create a dynamic motivational English teaching classroom by bringing together four motivation teaching components: teaching approach (POA), teaching tool (multimodality), teaching/learning organization (collaborative learning) as well as the motivational strategies in order to grasp the multifaceted nature of language learning motivation from different perspectives of L2 teaching. In this integrative framework, the three essential teaching elements cooperate and interact with each other, while motivational strategies selected from a combination of Dörnyei' s L2MSS and motivational teaching practice run through the beginning and end of the whole teaching process from the initial arousal of the motivation to the completion and evaluation of the motivated action, logically corresponding with the three phrases of motivating, enabling, and assessing in the language teaching process. Different teaching phases together with the embedding teaching organization and tool are filled with and guided by different motives, together achieving a systematic and enduring positive learning effect, as shown in Figure 3.1.

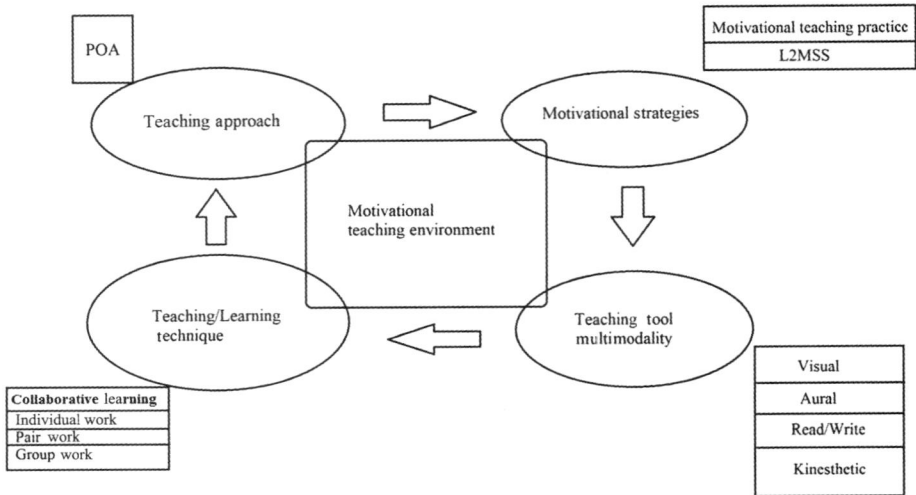

Figure 3.1 The Operational Framework of the Dynamic Motivational Teaching Model

3.4.1 Characteristic of the Dynamic Motivational Teaching Model

This model intends to create a pleasant and motivational environment in the teaching process, with the teaching method, teaching organization, teaching tools and motivational strategies cooperating together to facilitate the initiating and maintaining students' motivation throughout the whole foreign language classroom learning process.

As learning is believed to be enhanced through the act of producing language, which, by its mechanisms, increases the likelihood that learners become sensitive to what they can and cannot say in the target language (Shinichi Izumi, 2002), this model takes the language productive activity as the end as well as the driving force to realize the construction of the students' knowledge and the cultivation of their ability through the interaction between students and the relevant output tasks.

Starting from the key role of input enabling played in helping students to perform their output task, this teaching model is intended to make full use of various modal resources (such as language, vision, hearing, gesture, spatial mode and PPT, etc.), as well as a variety of media means (such as blackboard, computer, QQ group, Superstar Learning APP, etc.), to create a lively learning environment to stimulate students' interest and enthusiasm to participate in the learning process. It is believed that when students choose the materials and methods that suit their needs to support them to accomplish the output task, so their autonomous learning ability can gradually develop.

Featuring the task-based and activity-oriented, this teaching model adopts techniques of cooperative learning, in which students are active participants in the process of learning and producing through small group structures, working together to gain and maximize their own and each other's comprehension and production of the target language.

The following is a detailed account of how to implement these motivating components in the instruction design.

3.4.2 Multimodal Teaching

The reconstruction of English classroom teaching strategies from the perspective of multimodal learning in this research has been displayed in the following three aspects. First, in the motivating phase, the teacher adopted the modern multimedia technology to carry out her teaching online before the classroom teaching, so as to save more time for the next teaching process (Wen, 2015). Specifically speaking, the teacher employed the latest information technology—Superstar Learning APP, an information education software based on big data technology. Via this software, the researcher could upload the unit course material package, including the self-made curriculum chapter, related MOOC link, language point video, quizzes, etc. With the study materials, the production task and the evaluation criteria, students had a clear idea from beginning which elements of their performance and production would be appreciated (Dörnyei, 2001). The production task was presented in the form of mini-lecture to create a real-life communication scenario so that students can feel the existence of the actual context (Wen, 2015). When students learned the materials and received the production task arranged by the teacher, they completed the pre-class practice and made an attempt to produce the output task in the multimodal forms such as text, video, recording, etc. Then the teacher checked how well students learned the course materials by assessing the completion of quizzes through the learning platform, and collected the common problems of students. The amount of homework before class was generally small and not too difficult.

Then comes the enabling phase. In the classroom teaching stage, the teacher instructed students to carry out the selective learning in terms of language, content and structure. To make the input efficient and effective and the class engaging, various teaching modes should be adopted, such as PPT which can integrate the image, sound, animation into one, as well as other non-verbal behaviours, such as teachers' eye contact, gestures and movements, etc. In addition to these traditional teaching modes, Superstar Learning APP with diverse interactional functions can also serve the classroom teaching. For example, the teacher employed the check-in module of the learning platform to check students' attendance via gesture, positioning or QR code. When the teacher wanted to enlist students' answers or ideas, "cloud map brainstorming" could be used where students entered words through their smartphone in the teacher's prepared section. All these activities could be projected into the screen to focus students' attention and enhance students' enthusiasm for learning. After class, the teachers could also use Superstar Learning APP to set up the unit related online discussion to consolidate what was just learned in the classroom or provoked students' thought in preparation for the next class.

Third, in the phase of students and teacher collaborative assessment, the multimodality lies in the production work produced by students which were in different modes, for instance, the written work, like the composition or speech; the oral work, like presentation, role play, interview, and the video and recording made by students. While students carried out group task assignment, and made speech preparation and PPT, the teacher should appear as students' learning partner in the preparation process of student unit production work, giving advice and guidance. With the inclusive Superstar Learning APP, apart from the "cloud map brainstorming" function where the teacher and students can set up the criterion together, as well as evaluate students' work together, another function "voting" could also be used in this phase, where the teacher can invite all of the students in the class to assess, vote or grade other group's production works, by doing which the students would avoid sitting passively and being bored, and at the same time they would be more concentrated on listening to other group' work and can learn from their peers' advantages.

While adopting the multimodel teaching means, two things should be paid attention to. On the one hand, it advocates the use of multiple means such as text, sound, image, network and other modes to fully activate students' various senses to arouse students' enthusiasm in learning, so as to achieve the best teaching effect. On the other hand, when designing, selecting and coordinating all kinds of modes, the teacher should not blindly pursue innovation and interesting while neglecting the purpose of using teaching modes. Instead, they should serve the students' production task in terms of language, content and structure so as to maximize the teaching effect and help the students with their production work.

3.4.3 Collaborative Learning

As introduced previously, this teaching model adopts collaborative learning as the teaching organization technique to improve students' L2 language learning and communicative ability through the teacher-student and peer-peer communication and interaction. As to how to organize and administer this teaching organization in this motivational model to gain the maximal learning effects, it can be divided into two phases: preparatory phase and implementation phase. In the preparatory phase, the first thing to consider is group division and generally there are two major ways of doing this. One is that the teacher sets group rules in advance and assigns each group in terms of the principle of heterogeneous nature; the other is random combination, where students choose their favourite classmates or group with others randomly according to their seats (Li & Gong, 2019). In this study, the learners were grouped in the unit of dormitory of 4–6 students for the following consideration: Being in the same dormitory and free from the limitation of time and space, it was easier for them to get together and conduct a discussion at any time. In addition, students' fixed and free combination (a survey conducted on the first day of this semester among students showed that they were more willing to collaborate with their dorm mates as a learning group) can reduce students' anxiety, and create a relaxed and pleasant environment, so as to improve the quality of students' interaction both in and outside of classroom. Furthermore, compared to the randomly collected group, the students' fixed group was more likely to form a positive interdependence, that is, learners realized that the task can only be accomplished by combining his or her own effort with that of the other team members. This can increase the cohesion of the group to a certain extent, which has a significant positive correlation with the group's performance (Xu & Cao, 2012).

After several learning groups were formed, each member in a group was designated a particular role to play, including: a leader (to host the group discussion and to make sure that each member was on task by participating in the discussion or any given task), recorder (to take notes during the discussion), reporter (to report the summary of his/her group's discussion to the class), checker (to make sure that each one in the group finish the worksheet or to assign task in class), timer (to control the time given to their group and make sure that the assigned task was completed in time) or observer. But the role was not fixed, team members rotated to different roles in varying tasks in order to avoid the occurrence of free riders or possible complaint of overloading from some above-achievers. In general, one student played one role, and considering the number of students of a group and the difficulty and need of a task, sometimes a student played two roles, or a role was played by several students. No matter in what way, the division of assignment should be clear and specific, in order to facilitate the efficient collaborative learning.

The third thing should be considered before the implementation of collaborative learning is to develop the group norm. For example, the following requirements must be observed by team members: English is the only used language; listen carefully to the speeches of peers; do not talk about unrelated topics; all team members have responsibility to help each other to achieve common goals; mutual respect and trust; to often reflect on their performance in group activities; to build a sense of solidarity in cooperation, and so on.

Although coming from the same dormitory, they were freshmen just entered the university and may not be acquainted with each other when the study began. More importantly, due to the rare opportunity to speak a foreign language before, these learners may find embarrassed and not be willing to speak English with their peer in English. Therefore, to facilitate the quick and smooth processing of collaborative learning, it was necessary to carry out a team-building activity so as to turn these freshmen with diverse backgrounds and experiences into cooperative and caring team members. Here, a technique called Three-Step Interview was first employed to get the team members more acquainted with each other. In the Three-Step Interview, students take turns interviewing each other and then report what they learn to another pair. The three steps in this study were (1) Students A interviewed students for a required amount of time to learn their hometown, graduation high school, their hobbies and feelings about English learning; (2) at a signal, students changed roles and B interviewed A for the same amount of time; (3) at another signal, A and B each approached another pair, C and D, introducing and highlighting their partner's responses for Students C and D, and vice versa.

In the implementation stage, as discussed previously, collaborative learning in this teaching model involves the cooperation between teacher and students as well as among students. Employing in the three teaching procedures of the POA, it was implemented as followed: In the first phase of motivating, after the teacher presented the communicative scenes, the group members learned together and conducted a grouped topic discussion about how they were going to complete the task. They then tried producing output tasks in the form of individual or group work according to teachers' requirement and check each other's work. For the part of teacher, in order to diagnose students' difficulty in performing the assigned task and decide how much and what kind of information input is to be provided to the students, the teacher on the one hand, should have adequate exchanges with students to get effective feedbacks, and this could be achieved through the teacher-student interaction online, for example, through the QQ group, Wechat group or Superstar Learning APP, and on the other hand by checking the quality of each group's first output try, the teacher got to understand the students' existing knowledge, the mismatch and gap with the teaching objective.

In the enabling phase, the techniques used for collaborative learning involve (1) Think-Pair-Share; (2) Adapted Jigsaw Reading; (3) Round Robin Story Make-up; (4) Student Team Achievement Division. Think-Pair-Share was particularly effective as a warm-up for a whole class discussion in the beginning of one unit, where after the teacher posed a question, students thought individually for a few minutes, and then discussed and compared their responses with a partner before sharing with the entire class. For the second technique, though we can know from the previous introduction that the POA expects students to be equipped with relevant ideas, language expressions, or discourse structures to complete the assigned productive activity, teachers should never dominate the floor to present all the content by themselves, but give students' initiative into full play, giving them more opportunities to share teaching and learning responsibilities in class. Thus, an adapted collaborative learning of reciprocal teaching—Adapted Jigsaw Reading was adopted, instead of making students passive listeners, advocating a student-centered method, emphasizing students' involvement, participation and responsibility. In the Adapted Jigsaw Reading, the teacher divided the learning material into several parts, and each group was charged with developing expertise on one part, or on different components needed by students for production purpose, say, information synthesizing, language building and key discourse structure learning. Group members with a designated task learned together to master their task before class (each group can subdivide their task, with each member focusing on separate portions of the material and became an "expert" on his or her assigned portion, then he or she taught the other members of the home group). They also determined ways to help students get a good command of the material, exploring possible explanations, examples, illustrations and application, then in the class, group members with a specific task served as experts to teach the material, raise questions and elicit answers and finally to conduct quiz test. During and after the Adapted Jigsaw Reading, another technique could be used in this teaching model was Student Team Achievement Division, where after each unit learning, each student could contribute to their team score by his or her improvement score comparing to his previous unit score, and the team total score was the sum of each member's improvement score. The score was counted through a combination of their performance in class activity and on unit quizzes. In order to earn points in the two items above, students were encouraged to focus attention and participate actively in class and exert themselves in consolidating what they had learned, so that they were able to earn them points which would also determine their team scores (Slavin, 1995). In this way, students would not only work hard themselves but also help others to perform better in the quiz in order for a total high group score, therefore, both individual accountability and the team contingency got improved. The quiz that students took in this model involved the language expressions and key sentences closely related to or serving for their production work. The last technique that was occasionally utilized was called Round Robin Story Make-up, in which different groups took turns to brainstorm and create a new story ending.

In the assessment phase, or teacher and students collaborative assessment, to be exact, according to the POA, cooperation can be displayed establishing assessing criterion between teacher and students and peer editing among students. For the cooperation between teacher and students, after students submitted their products, taking the production of writing as an example, the teacher and students evaluated the typical products of one or two students' collaboratively in class. The teacher showed his or her revision and asked students to undertake a discussion in pair to find out why the writing should be revised like this. When the teacher helped students understand how to identify the features of good and poor writing in the work of others, students' critical evaluation skills developed which they could apply to their own writing. Thus, the collaborative assessment between students and teacher could be considered as a training and guidance for students on how to critically reviewing and providing editorial feedbacks on each other's work. After the class, students exchanged their production with their partners, carried out peer editing and expected constructive criticism from their partners so that they could improve their papers before they finally submitted their work to the teacher.

3.4.4 Motivational Strategies

As mentioned in Chapter 2, the motivation-enhancing strategies in this study were grounded in a combination of Motivational Teaching Practice in the L2 Classrooms framework (Dörnyei, 2001) and L2MSS (Dörnyei, 2009), both of which were presented in the form of activities and naturally woven into the ordinary teaching content and teaching processes to increase student motivation and meet the course goals. The main activities aiming to improve the ideal self in this study were based on the six elements required for L2 selves to exert their full motivational capacity (Dörnyei, 2009) and the training programme by Magid and Chan (2012). The interventional treatment can be implemented with the following steps.

Step1: According to Dörnyei (2009), the precondition of self-motivation function of ideal self is that they "need to exist", so in the first week of the experimental teaching, after highlighting the role that the L2 played in the world and how knowing the L2 could be potentially useful for the students, the researcher had students discuss in group their role models and brainstorm on their L2 connected ideal self. Then they were asked to submit their "Ideal L2 Self" written report as a writing assignment, in which they were required to visualize situations where they could efficiently use the L2 or contact with L2 speakers in their future jobs and personal life. They were encouraged to describe their future possible self the more elaborate and vivid, the better.

Step 2: Instruct students to identify their immediate goal and action plans in order to operationalize their ideal L2 self. As a goal is a dream or hope with a deadline, and a plan illustrates how a person will achieve the goals with specific steps and actions that will take (Hock et al., 2002). Students were asked set their short-term goals and long-term goal with a timeline and indicated when they expected to achieve their goals, then concrete action plans to achieve these goals were asked to be developed. As with other classroom activities, while doing this, collaborative learning was also adopted in which students were first asked to think independently for 10 minutes, then they carried out a group discussion followed by a group representative as a model chosen by the researcher to share their immediate goal and specific action plans to the whole class. Finally, the students were asked to submit their reports as another writing assignment.

Step 3: Students were asked to monitor their plan fulfilment, assess their progress on the action plans and to revise action plans regularly to help students stay focused on their action plan.

Dörnyei and Kubanyiova (2014) emphasize target vision building in class should be consistently and frequently use as a general part of the motivational teaching practice of L2 teachers. To consolidate the previous activity effect and keep students' ideal self fresh, in the middle of the semester, the research-instructor also drew on an ideal L2 self-video recording task (Erdil, 2016) to enhance students' ideal L2 self. In this task, students were required to imagine themselves few years later when they became a successful person and were invited by the researcher to record a video to motivate and give advice to her current demotivated students to learn a second language.

Besides the specifically designed activities to facilitate students to construct their ideal L2 self which can in turn enhance L2 learning motivation, as a matter of fact, using imagery to address students' L2 ideal self targeting the overall L2 learning motivation did not limit to the specific designed project, rather, in each unit of the teaching course, the motivating phase of the POA providing students with guided imagery of situations where L2 was efficiently used by the learners could also function as the target vision building strategies to help to enhance students' visualization of their ideal L2 speaker self who can effectively use English to do things and communicate with native speakers.

As indicated by Dörnyei (2001), a few well-chosen strategies that suit both the teacher and their learners are enough in creating a positive motivational climate in the classroom rather than using every one of the long of strategies, therefore, based on motivational teaching practice (Dörnyei, 2001) and strategy log by Erdil (2016), and after a reflection on the strategies which may work and ones that may not work according to the characteristics of the students at the research setting and the teaching goals, the researcher finally established her strategy log to integrate them into the course lessons as shown in Table 3.4.

Table 3.4 Motivational Strategy Repertory

Time	Content	Motivational strategy in classroom
1–2 weeks	Introductory session (an introduction to the subject of English in college as well as the motivational teaching model)	1. Highlighting the role that the L2 plays in the world 2. Highlighting how knowing the L2 can be potentially useful for the students 3. Demonstrating and talking about my own enthusiasm for the course material, and how it affects me personally 4. Sharing with students that you value English as a meaningful experience 5. Helping to create realistic learner beliefs by raising the learners' general awareness about how languages should be learned and the factors that can contribute to success 6. Telling students what the criteria for success of this course involves

3–13 weeks	1–5 units' course learning	7. Individual presentation (at the beginning of the class for 2–3 minutes)/warming up 8. Clearly stating unit objectives, drawing attention from time to time to the objectives and how particular materials and activities help to attain them 9. Creating a pleasant & supportive atmosphere (smiley face, understanding tone of voice, encouraging risk-taking and having mistakes accepted as a natural part of learning) 10. Making learning stimulating and enjoyable for the learners 11. Using goal-setting for every unit by breaking down tasks and assignments into small steps, emphasizing goal completion deadlines and offering ongoing feedbacks 12. Explaining the purpose and utility of the task 13. Making task content attractive by adapting it to the students' natural interests and making the teaching materials relevant to the students 14. Enlisting students as active task participants 15. Using competitive methods to encourage students to submit the assignment as early as possible 16. Increasing the amount of English you use in the class 17. Encouraging students to use English outside the classroom 18. Inviting English-speaking foreigners to class 19. Promoting exposure to L2 cultural products like authentic materials (e.g. videos) 20. Breaking the monotony of classroom events by use of technology, outside materials, humor, videos, music 21. Using individual work/pair work/group work alternatively, followed by a share with the whole class 22. Including information-gap and problem-solving activities for which students pair up to cooperatively complete a meaningful and challenging task 23. Making sure that they receive sufficient preparation and assistance 24. Making sure that there are no serious obstacles to success 25. Making tasks attractive by including novel and fantasy elements 26. Promoting learner autonomy by handing over as much as you can of the various leadership/teaching roles and functions to the learners and being the facilitator of the learning process 27. Protecting the learners' self-esteem and increasing their confidence by providing learners with encouragement, teaching them various learner strategies and helping diminishes their language anxiety 28. Showing students that you care about their progress

14th week	Conclusion, reflection and prepare students for the final examination	29. Encouraging learners to explain their failures by the lack of effort and appropriate strategies applied rather than by their insufficient abilities 30. Raising students' awareness of the importance of self-motivation 31. Making sure that grades also reflect effort and improvement and not just objective levels of achievement 32. Telling students the exact format of the forthcoming final test, types of question and the evaluation criteria

3.4.5 The POA

As stated before, the POA is composed of three processes in the foreign language teaching practice, the following Table 3.5 would specify how the integration of the POA and other three components interplay with each other in each phase as the teaching activity progresses.

Table 3.5 The Operationalization of the Dynamic Motivational Teaching Model

Phase	Content	Multimodality	Collaborative learning	Motivational strategies
Motivating	Teachers present the communicative scenes.	Mini-lecture online	/	Making the teaching materials and the unit task relevant to the students by relating the subject matter to everyday experiences and backgrounds of the learners
	Students try producing the output tasks.	Written work/ presentation/ role play/ interview recorded video	Group learning and checking together	Creating realistic learner beliefs
	Teachers announce teaching aims and the output tasks.	PPT	Individual accountability	Increasing the learners' goal-orientedness

Enabling	Teachers divide the general output tasks into several small ones, and provide learning materials and guidance accordingly.	PPT text/video /listening materials	Individual accountability	Increasing the learners' expectancy of success in particular tasks by providing sufficient preparation and offering assistance
	Students select the content, language and structure to learn which are closely relevant to the output to be produced from the materials given by the teacher.	Text/video /listening materials	Think-Pair-Share/Jigsaw Reading (Text understanding/ vocabulary/ writing skill) / Round Robin Story Make-up	Making learning stimulating and enjoyable; Increasing the students' motivation by actively promoting learner autonomy
	Students produce the output tasks.	Written work/ presentation/ role play/ interview recorded video	After finishing their assignment independently, students submit them in group	Increasing students' goal-orientedness by drawing students' attention from time to time to unit goals
Assessing	The teacher and students learn the assessment criteria together.	PPT	Teacher and students collaborate together	Making sure that they know exactly that success in the task involves
	Students submit their product to the teacher.	Online written work/ presentation/ role play/ interview recorded video	After finishing their assignment independently, students submitted them in group	Taking into account team products and not just individual products in your assessments
	The teacher and students evaluate students' product collaboratively.	PPT	Students first evaluate individually and then make a group discussion	Providing motivational feedback; Including problem-solving activities that lead to the successful completion of whole-group tasks or small-group tasks

3.5 Collection of Data

This study began in the autumn 2020 at the researcher's university in China and spanned across 14 weeks with data collection administered at different stages. In the first week, the initial questionnaire data and the previous written and oral test results were collected, in the 13rd week, the post-test were administered and collected; in the 14th week, the same questionnaire was used and the semi-structured interview conducted; the self-reports were gathered twice, in the 3rd week after the complete of the first unit of the course and in the 14th week respectively. In the following section, how these instruments mentioned above contributed to answering the research questions will be explained.

3.5.1 Data Collection for Research Question 1

Q1. What are the effects of the dynamic motivational teaching model on the L2 learners' motivation toward learning English?

Both quantitative and qualitative data were used to answer this question. The quantitative data was Students' L2 Motivational Questionnaire which was used repeatedly to collect data prior to and after the experimental teaching. The purpose of the same questionnaire administered at different time slots was that the initial data intended to know the motivational status quo of the freshmen learning a second language, and the second one obtained with this instrument seeked to figure out if there was any significant difference of students in their English learning motivation compared with their previous one after the teaching treatment. The qualitative data was students' self-reports which were collected twice. While the first one was used to collect students' initial feeling, questions and difficulty concerning the dynamic teaching model, and was mainly aimed to improve the researcher's teaching, the second one which was anonymously gathered was used to cross-check the validation of the data from the questionnaire to examine students' motivation intensity.

In order to make sure that the subjects took the questionnaires seriously, students were asked to fill in these questionnaires in the normal class time with a time limit of 20 minutes when their teachers were present. To avoid any potential influence that writing down their names may bring to their responses, the participants were told to feel free to choose what they thought were true because the questionnaire was anonymous and confidential. Detailed instructions were given to help the participants to get a clear idea about what they were expected to do. Whenever students encountered any problems concerning the questionnaire, the researcher was at hand to help them out. After the questionnaire sheets were amassed, those that were not complete or from students who randomly chose the same item for different questions were considered of no avail and were abandoned, therefore, there were altogether 125 questionnaire sheets collected from the students in both the experimental and control group for analysis.

3.5.2 Data Collection for Research Question 2

Q2. What are the effects of the dynamic motivational teaching model on the improvement of the L2 learners' English language proficiency?

Oral tests and written tests at the beginning and toward the end of the semester were contributed to answering the question. The purpose of the two types of tests was to find out whether this teaching model helped to make a difference in students' L2 academic achievements.

The initial written test was conducted in the first week of the semester as the pre-test followed by the oral test in the second week, while the second written and oral administered in the 13th week as the post-test. As discussed in the sample part, in order to keep the confidentiality of the test content, a total of 42 participants with 14 students from each level of proficiency: high, medium and low participated in the examinations. Students from both the experimental group and the control group took part in the examinations at the same time, and in the oral test, examinees were scrambly allocated in four examination rooms, which means that each test room consisted of participants of three diverse levels of English proficiency.

3.5.3 Piloting and Adaptation of the Dynamic Motivational Teaching Model

The teaching model was piloted with one unit from the course book with 30 non-English major volunteers. The pilot teaching extended 4 sessions, 8 periods of classes, altogether 360 minutes in the winter 2019 at the researcher's university. There were two objectives in the piloting of the teaching model. The first one was to examine whether the motivational teaching model could be positively accepted by the L2 learners; the second was to gain experience for the better implementation of the teaching model for the following formal teaching experiment. The learners' class performance and their self report after the piloting indicated that, in general, the teaching model was warmly welcomed by the learners. However, there also existed some problems, for example, due to time limit, it was difficult to spend sufficient time both on teaching students' knowledge useful for their tasks and on the assessment of students' multiple subtasks output and unit production. In order to solve the dilemma and make good use of class time, a kind of flipped classroom was introduced in this course where students learned the text-related background, text analysis and key words and expressions online before class, while leaving time for the knowledge closely related to and serving for their production task and assessment. Additionally, it was found during the piloting classroom that while a student or group made a presentation, some other students did not pay attention on the presentation. In order to get all students actively involved in the class so that they would not get bored and can learn from other students' performance, the researcher initiated the classroom operation function of Superstar Learning APP, where all students participated in the voting and rating of the reporters via their smart phones. Still another, as the unit production task was further divided into several subtasks, and students were faced with more homework than they expected it should be in college, it was hard to require students to complete each task every time effectively and submit their work efficiently, especially the group work. In view of the problem, the researcher launched a competitive mechanism that the last group submitting their work had to give a performance (sing or dance) to entertain other groups. All of these adaptations were proved to achieve a good effect in the subsequent experimental study (see Appendix G for a model teaching plan).

3.5.4 Data Collection for Research Question 3

Q3. What are the effects of the dynamic motivational teaching model on the high, medium and low achievers in a heterogeneous class?

To figure out the impact of the teaching model on students of diverse English academic achievements, data from the written and oral test results were also collected to answer this research question.

In order to avoid the Hawthorne Effect, that is, students may provide answers or opinions against their real feelings to please their teacher in their work (questionnaire and self-report), and to get rid of students' apprehension about their test scores, the participants were convinced that these data collected were only used in a study, to help teachers improve teaching skills and better serve the students. Students showed their understanding, and when the researcher requested their permission to use it for research purposes at the end of the course, all participants consented.

3.6 Data Analysis

The data collected for analysis to examine the effectiveness of the dynamic motivational teaching model in this study involved (1) the results of the motivational questionnaire; (2) students' self-reports; (3) the scores of the pre and post written test; and (4) the scores of the pre and post oral test.

The quantitative analysis involved the questionnaire data and the written and oral test scores. After the 6-point Likert scale questionnaire sheets were collected, all the data were entered into a computer. Questions in the first three sections—attitudes toward the course, linguistic self-confidence, ideal L2 self—were asked from the positive point of view (e.g. I enjoy learning English.), which meant the higher the score, the stronger students' L2 motivation, but questions in the fourth section—L2 anxiety were asked from the negative point of view (e.g. I hate English.), which meant the low score representing the high degree of motivation in acquiring the language. However, for the sake of calculation convenience of the students' overall motivation, all the negative codes were subjected to be recoded to the positive ones. That is, the original datum 6 (strongly disagree) was transformed into 1 (strongly agree), 5 (disagree) into 2 (agree), 4 (somewhat disagree) into 3 (somewhat agree), 3 into 4, 2 into 5 and 1 into 6, so such questions would score 1 point, 2 points, 3 points, 4 points, 5 point and 6 points corresponding to the answers of "strongly agree", "agree", "somewhat agree", "somewhat disagree", "disagree" and "strongly disagree". The total score of each item was calculated via SPSS17.0, which was followed by a standard score. Then the score of each item was ordered through ascending sorting according to the standard score. Data with scores higher than 2 and less than 2 were invalid (data higher than 2 times standard deviation in normal distribution) and eliminated. Then statistics yielded with the help of SPSS were compared for the inter- and intra-group descriptive analysis. The Independent Samples t-test was run for the inter-group analysis of the data collected from both the experimental group and the control group, while the Paired Samples Test for the intra-group analysis of the data collected before and after the treatment. Pilot study had carried out in the first place by using Independent t-test and Cronbach's Alpha coefficient to test the internal consistency of the questionnaire items.

For the examination of students' language proficiency, two teacher raters were recruited to score the written test and the oral test with the researcher. They learned the score descriptors together for the subjective items (translation and writing) of the written test papers, then they selected 4–5 test papers as models, scored and compared, and finally reached the agreed scores and set the tune for the following independent large-size scoring. The oral test scoring also followed the same process. The final score of the repeated oral test and the subjective part of written test of each student was the average of the three raters. After the grades came out, statistical software SPSS was also utilized to analyse the data to compare the inter- and intra-group differences. The *t*-test, independent samples test and paired sample statistics were reported to figure out whether there was significant difference between the two groups in the oral and written test before and after the experimental teaching.

For the qualitative data, students' self-reports, data from the E-Learning platform where students turned in was downloaded and printed by the researcher, who then numbered them from Student 1 to Student 63. One colleague teacher, also a Ph.D. candidate was invited to be an inter-rater and made the data analysis with the researcher, and they made an agreement to process the data in the following stages. First, they started with several times of reading to get themselves familiarized with the data, then they located any information relevant to the learners' changes in their L2 learning motivation. Next, they classified the information and color-coded them manually. Then they made a meeting and reached a consensus to divide the data into three broad categories: (1) overall feelings over the dynamic motivational teaching model, (2) students' gains in this semester's English learning; and (3) students' favorite activities in this semester's English course. After that, relevant information of each category was located, classified and coded by the two raters independently. Finally, the researcher looked for the common themes between them, for example, in terms of students' gains in this semester's English learning, the same recurring themes across all the students' self-reports shared by the two raters were the enhanced confidence, strengthened friendship and the improvement in speaking and writing, etc. Besides, they also agreed that new codes were open to be added with further reading and more interaction with the data. (Lincoln & Guba, 1985) Once the themes were finalized by them, the researcher made a table (Table 3.6) to set patterns with some descriptions of each theme.

Table 3.6 Summary of the Research Process

Research objective	Source of data or sample	Data collection method or research instrument	Method of data analysis	Expected results
To investigate the effectiveness of the dynamic motivational English teaching model on the EFL learners' motivation toward learning English as a foreign language	Stage I: Freshmen students of various non-English majors from a provincial key university, China, were grouped into two classes through the university course online selective system.	·Student L2 Motivational Questionnaire ·Self-report	·Mean &*SD* ·Independent Sample *t*-test ·Descriptive analysis ·Content analysis	The students in the experimental group are expected to have a higher motivational status towards English learning than the students in the control group.
To find out the effectiveness of the dynamic motivational English teaching model on the improvement of the EFL learners' language proficiency in terms of the oral and written examination	Stage II: The students constituted two classes, with each of 60–70 students, one was designated as the experimental group and the other the control group.	·Oral examination ·Written examination	·Mean ·*SD* ·*t*-test	The students in the experimental group are anticipated to have a higher score in their oral and written exam than the students in the control group.
To study the effectiveness of the motivational English teaching model based on the POA on the high/medium/low achievers in a heterogeneous class	Stage III: The students were divided into high, medium, and low achievers based on their English scores in the entrance examination.	·Oral examination ·Written examination ·Students' self-reports	·*t*-test ·Content analysis	The results are expected to show that the influence of the teaching model is different on students of diverse English academic achievements.

Chapter 4 Research Findings

This study has attempted to investigate the effectiveness of a motivational teaching model in EFL teaching in college, the results of the questionnaire, the interview, self-report and oral and written test with regard to the three questions formulated in the research: (1) the effects of the motivational teaching model on the EFL learners' motivation toward learning English as a foreign language; (2) the effects of the motivational teaching model on the improvement of the EFL learners' language proficiency; (3) the effects of the motivational teaching model on the high/medium/low achievers in a heterogeneous class.

The following space will see the results presented in the order of the research questions stated above.

4.1 Effects of the Motivational Teaching Model on the EFL Learners' Motivation

In this research, both the experimental group and the control group were required to complete a questionnaire on L2 learning motivation prior to and after the experimental teaching to investigate the effects of the teaching model on the students' motivational state toward learning English as a foreign language. The questionnaire was a 6-point Likert scale. The higher marks learners scored, the more intensified their L2 learning motivation displayed. The degree of motivation intensity was divided into six levels—very high, high, moderate high, moderate low, low and very low. For the first three factors from the positive point of view, the high marks were also interpreted positively, but for the fourth factor with negative expression, the high marks meant the low level of anxiety as shown in Table 4.1.

Table 4.1 Intensity Scale of Motivation Scores in L2MQ

Mean score	Interpretation (F1, F2, F3/F4)	Interval
1–1.84	Very low/Very high	0.84
1.85–2.67	Low/High	0.83
2.68–3.50	Moderate low/Moderate high	0.83
3.51–4.33	Moderate high/Moderate low	0.83
4.34–5.16	High/Low	0.83
5.17–6	Very high/Very low	0.84

Table 4.2 below shows the mean scores and the corresponding motivational level of each item under the three factors on the L2 motivation questionnaire data from both the experimental group and the control group at two different time periods: prior to and after the treatment.

Table 4.2 Levels of Students' Motivation Intensity in Each Item of
L2MQ of Two Groups

Descriptions	Tests	Experimental group			Control group		
		Mean	SD	Interpretation	Mean	SD	Interpretation
Factor 1 (Attitudes Toward the Course)							
1. I am looking forward to our English class.	Pre	3.76	1.126	Moderate high	3.74	1.20	Moderate high
	Post	3.76	0.97	Moderate high	3.58	1.017	Moderate high
2. I am attentive to what the teacher says in English class.	Pre	4.23	0.931	Moderate high	4.27	1.058	Moderate high
	Post	4.27	0.89	Moderate high	4.23	0.965	Moderate high

3. I like to speak English in English class.	Pre	3.74	1.20	Moderate high	3.44	1.236	Moderate low
	Post	4.10	0.882	Moderate high	3.60	1.152	Moderate high
4. I am very happy whenever we have English class.	Pre	3.73	1.011	Moderate high	3.74	1.173	Moderate high
	Post	4.60	1.016	High	3.97	1.228	Moderate high
5. I study English because I like it, not for the sake of passing exams or tests.	Pre	3.89	1.147	Moderate high	3.81	1.212	Moderate high
	Post	3.95	0.931	Moderate high	3.50	1.067	Moderate low

Factor 2 (Linguistic Self-Confidence)

1. I feel that I can make progress in English.	Pre	4.21	1.073	Moderate high	4.02	1.248	Moderate high
	Post	4.18	0.878	Moderate high	3.79	1.203	Moderate high
2. I think that I can learn English well, if I try hard enough.	Pre	5.03	0.975	High	4.98	1.032	High
	Post	5.16	0.706	High	4.74	1.173	High
3. I often experience a feeling of success in my English lessons.	Pre	3.61	1.15	Moderate high	3.89	1.103	Moderate high
	Post	4.50	1.098	High	3.60	1.152	Moderate high
4. I am sure that one day I will be able to speak English well.	Pre	4.97	1.116	High	4.92	1.076	High
	Post	5.00	0.868	High	3.92	1.106	Moderate high
5. In English lessons, I usually understand what to do and how to do it.	Pre	3.77	1.015	Moderate high	4.11	0.994	Moderate high
	Post	4.21	0.96	Moderate high	3.97	1.228	Moderate high
6. This semester, I think I will be good at learning English.	Pre	3.58	1.124	Moderate high	3.87	0.949	Moderate high
	Post	4.15	0.884	Moderate high	4.02	1.094	Moderate high

7. I often volunteer to answer questions in English lessons.	Pre	3.18	1.094	Moderate low	2.95	1.151	Moderate low
	Post	4.00	1.086	Moderate high	3.18	1.124	Moderate low
Factor 3 (Ideal L2 Self)							
1. I can imagine myself writing English e-mails/ letters fluently.	Pre	3.71	1.206	Moderate high	3.94	1.054	Moderate high
	Post	3.92	1.076	Moderate high	3.53	1.211	Moderate high
2. I can imagine myself living abroad and having a discussion in English.	Pre	3.74	0.904	Moderate high	4.27	1.058	Moderate high
	Post	3.92	1.135	Moderate high	3.23	1.286	Moderate low
3. I can imagine myself studying in a university where all my courses are taught in English.	Pre	3.58	1.124	Moderate high	3.66	1.039	Moderate high
	Post	3.35	1.243	Moderate low	3.03	1.355	Moderate low
4. I can imagine a situation where I am speaking English with foreigners.	Pre	4.45	0.862	High	3.68	1.083	Moderate high
	Post	4.60	0.983	High	3.90	1.339	Moderate high
5. I can imagine myself speaking English with international friends or colleagues.	Pre	4.10	1.277	Moderate high	3.95	1.093	Moderate high
	Post	4.27	0.995	Moderate high	3.79	1.042	Moderate high
6. Whenever I think of my future career, I imagine myself using English	Pre	3.74	1.267	Moderate high	3.94	1.304	Moderate high
	Post	4.48	0.987	High	4.21	1.088	Moderate high
Grand mean	Pre	3.95	1.089	Moderate high	3.95	1.115	Moderate high
	Post	4.25	0.977	Moderate high	3.77	1.157	Moderate high

There are altogether 5 variables loaded onto Factor 1 (attitudes toward the course), which address students' feelings about their current English class and course. The result of comparison between the pre-and post-treatment motivational questionnaire in the experimental group revealed that except for Item 1 which remained the same level in the post test with the previous one, all other 4 items witnessed a mean score increase, among which Item 4 (I am very happy whenever we have English class.) saw the remarkable improvement as the mean score increased from 3.73 to 4.60, and the level improved from "moderate high" to "high". This indicated that learners had a positive feeling toward this course and enjoyed the pleasant and relaxing classroom learning environment under the motivational teaching model. In contrast, of all the 5 items in this subscale, there were 3 items that the mean score (Item 1, Item 2, Item 5) saw a drop in the control group, for example, Item 5 "I study English because I like it, not for the sake of passing exams or tests." saw a noticeable decrease from 3.81 to 3.50, with the state level falling from "moderate high" to "moderate low". This indicated that students did not have positive attitudes to L2, and their motivation to learn the L2 was purely extrinsic.

Factor 2 (linguistic self-confidence) included 7 items which investigated students' perception of their ability to cope with L2 learning and achieve desired goals in terms of L2 proficiency (Guilloteaux & Dörnyei, 2008). As shown in Table 4.2, all the items loaded onto this factor experienced an increase in the mean score except Item 6, among which, Item 2 and Item 4, that is, "I think that I can learn English well, if I try hard enough." and "I am sure that one day I will be able to speak English well." saw the highest mean score in the post-test. This indicated that the semester's treatment experience boosted learners' self-confidence which convinced them that the mastery of L2 was well within his or her means and potentials (Clément et al., 1994). Item 3 "I often experience a feeling of success in my English lessons."

witnessed the biggest rise of the mean score from 3.61 to 4.50, which indicated that students were entitled to successful learning experiences under this motivational teaching model which enhanced their self-confidence. The control group, however, of all the 7 items related to linguistic self-confidence, 5 items (Item 1 to Item 5) showed a drop in the mean score in the post test, indicating the traditional L2 classroom lacked the incentive environment to boost students' L2 learning self-confidence, and students could not link themselves with competent L2 learners and users.

Factor 3 (ideal L2 self), consisting 6 items, assessed students' ability to imagine themselves as successful and proficient L2 speakers. As an important component of the L2MSS theory, this theme suggested that students' L2 motivation could be enhanced if they had a strong, detailed, vivid mental image of their ideal L2 self as a proficient L2 speaker (Dörnyei, 2005, 2009). The findings before and after the treatment in L2MQ showed that students had stronger ideal L2-related images of themselves who can write English email/letters fluently (Item 1), or live abroad and have a discussion in English (Item 2), or speak English with international friends or colleagues (Item 4), etc. This may due to the target vison building strategies which were consistently and frequently used in this study. As a sharp contrast, a majority of items in this section for the control group were subjected to a decrease in the mean score, which indicated that students in the regular class were not able to imagine themselves from who they were actually are (the actual self) and who they would likely to become (the ideal self), nor can they envision themselves as someone who can easily communicate in the L2 with confidence. (See Table 4.3 for details.)

Table 4.3   Levels of Students' L2 Use Anxiety of the Two Groups

Descriptions	Tests	Experimental group			Control group		
		Mean	*SD*	Interpretation	Mean	*SD*	Interpretation
Factor 4 (L2 Use Anxiety)							
1. I find English class very boring. I always feel sleepy in English class.	Pre	3.10	1.169	Moderate high	2.94	1.424	Moderate high
	Post	4.13	0.82	Moderate low	2.97	1.437	Moderate high
2. I get nervous and confused when I am speaking in my English class.	Pre	3.73	1.291	Moderate low	3.24	1.289	Moderate high
	Post	3.84	1.244	Moderate low	3.60	1.324	Moderate low
3. I am afraid that my classmates will laugh at me when I have to speak in English lessons.	Pre	3.09	1.464	Moderate high	2.68	1.566	Moderate high
	Post	4.21	0.813	Moderate low	2.84	1.517	Moderate high
4. I think it is very difficult to learn English.	Pre	3.19	1.238	Moderate high	3.66	1.039	Moderate low
	Post	4.23	0.948	Moderate low	3.45	1.351	Moderate high
5. I always feel that the other students speak English better than I do.	Pre	3.21	1.401	Moderate high	3.68	1.083	Moderate low
	Post	3.40	1.194	Moderate high	3.42	1.325	Moderate high
6. I hate English, but I have no choice. I just have to sit in class without any choice.	Pre	2.41	1.502	High	2.52	1.501	High
	Post	4.11	1.161	Moderate low	2.66	1.354	High

7. I am worried about my ability to do well in English.	Pre	3.35	1.368	Moderate high	3.16	1.381	Moderate high
	Post	4.39	1.03	Moderate low	3.18	1.409	Moderate high
8. I would rather spend time on subjects other than English.	Pre	3.44	1.21	Moderate high	3.34	1.173	Moderate high
	Post	4.26	0.904	Moderate low	3.32	1.052	Moderate high
Grand mean	Pre	3.19	1.330	Moderate high	3.15	1.307	Moderate high
	Post	4.07	1.014	Moderate low	3.18	1.346	Moderate high

The fourth factor was loaded onto "L2 Use Anxiety", referring to students' general level of anxiety when they had to use the L2 in and outside their class. Since the items in this part were negative statements about L2 use, and the interpretative levels were inverted, the analysis revealed that the students of both the experimental group and control group perceived a moderate high and high level of L2 anxiety in the pre survey with the grand mean of 3.19 and 3.15 respectively. After one semester of the dynamic motivation English teaching model, the findings showed a noticeable progress in the experimental group with the increasing grand mean at 4.07. When considering on each aspect, the highest improvement was on Item 6 "I hate English, but I have no choice. I just have to sit in class without any choice." saw the most noticeable progress. The perception of the experimental group changed significantly from high (2.41) to low anxiety (4.11). This indicated that the experimental group had more enjoyable learning experience during the treatment period, who thought that the English classroom was more supportive and had more confidence when they produced the target language. However, it was not the case for the control group. No sign of improvement as displayed in Table 4.3 can be found in the 8 items, which implied that the traditional teaching model had limited effect in reducing students' level of anxiety.

After the descriptive analysis, statistical *t*-tests were conducted to have a better understanding of the data. The inter- and the intra-group comparisons were made on the factor averages of the pre-and post-treatment motivational questionnaire. The first comparison was on the experimental group at two different time periods via paired samples *t*-tests.

In statistics, *p*-value is the criterion to determine whether the difference is significant. $p>0.05$ means there is no significant difference between the two groups; $p>0.01$ means the difference between the two groups is significant; $p<0.01$ means the difference between the two groups is quite significant and $p<0.001$ means the difference between the two groups is of extremely significance. As shown in Table 4.4, the experimental group gained a significant improvement in all of the four subscales and the overall motivation toward learning English in the post-treatment L2MQ with all the five *p*-values lower than 0.01 after one semester's intervention of teaching. That is to say, students in the experimental group progressed in all of the four factors constituted the L2 motivational questionnaire.

Table 4.4 Paired Samples Tests on Pre and Post L2MQ in Experimental Groups (*N*=62)

Items	Tests	Mean	*SD*	*t*-value	*p*-value
Factor 1	Pre	3.87	1.097	-3.299	0.001 **
	Post	4.14	0.948		
Factor 2	Pre	4.05	1.261	-6.006	0.000 ***
	Post	4.46	1.019		
Factor 3	Pre	3.81	1.195	-3.382	0.001 **
	Post	4.09	1.146		
Factor 4	Pre	3.19	1.357	-3.464	0.000 **
	Post	4.07	1.060		
Overall	Pre	3.69	1.294	-7.789	0.000 ***
	Post	4.19	1.066		

As a sharp contrast to the significant gains in the overall motivational intensity and each subscale in the experimental group, the control group, instead of making any improvement in the post-test, no significant difference can be identified in Factor 1 and Factor 4 with p-value >0.5. To make matters worse, their scores on the subscales of F2, F3 and the overall motivation dropped significantly in the post motivational questionnaire as all the three p-values<0.01 as shown in Table 4.5.

Table 4.5 Paired Samples Tests on Pre- and Post-Treatment L2MQ in Control Groups (N=62)

Items	Tests	Mean	SD	t-value	p-value
Factor 1	Pre	3.80	1.201	0.277	0.782
	Post	3.77	1.118		
Factor 2	Pre	4.11	1.252	2.887	0.004 **
	Post	3.89	1.228		
Factor 3	Pre	3.91	1.120	3.327	0.001 **
	Post	3.62	1.282		
Factor 4	Pre	3.15	1.369	-0.339	0.735
	Post	3.18	1.377		
Overall	Pre	3.71	1.308	2.608	0.009 **
	Post	3.58	1.300		

After the comparison between the pre- and post-treatment L2MQ of two groups, the inter-group differences in the students' motivation toward learning English were also compared via the Independent Samples Test. It can be found from Table 4.6, there was no significant difference between the two groups of students in any of the four factors towards English learning in the pre-test questionnaire (p<0.5).

Table 4.6 Independent Sample *t*-Test of Motivational Change in Pre-Test (*N* of Each Group=62)

Items	Groups	Mean	SD	*t*-value	*p*-value
Factor 1	Experimental	3.87	1.097	-0.733	0.464
	Control	3.80	1.201		
Factor 2	Experimental	4.05	1.261	-0.648	0.517
	Control	4.11	1.252		
Factor 3	Experimental	3.81	1.195	-1.140	0.255
	Control	3.91	1.120		
Factor 4	Experimental	3.19	1.357	0.396	0.695
	Control	3.15	1.369		
Overall	Experimental	3.69	1.294	-0.298	0.766
	Control	3.71	1.308		

However, after one semester's motivational teaching intervention, extreme significance was found between the experimental group and the control group ($p=0.00<0.001$) as demonstrated in Table 4.7. This indicated that the two groups of learners had the similar motivation to learn English when the experiment commenced, but the treatment group enhanced their L2 motivation to a larger extent than the control group did after one semester's motivational teaching modal treatment.

Table 4.7 Independent Sample *t*-Test of Motivational Change in Post-Test (*N* of Each Group=62)

Items	Groups	Mean	SD	*t*-value	*p*-value
Factor 1	Experimental	4.14	0.976	4.286	0.000 ***
	Control	3.77	1.118		
Factor 2	Experimental	4.46	1.019	7.428	0.000 ***
	Control	3.89	1.228		
Factor 3	Experimental	4.09	1.146	5.337	0.000 ***
	Control	3.62	1.282		
Factor 4	Experimental	4.07	1.060	11.418	0.000 ***
	Control	3.18	1.377		
Overall	Experimental	4.19	1.066	14.493	0.000 ***
	Control	3.58	1.300		

To sum up, the questionnaire administered in 2020 is a quantitative instrument to examine the effectiveness of the motivational teaching practice on students' L2 motivation. As a result, Paired Samples *t*-tests and Independent *t*-tests on the pre- and post-treatment L2MQ factor scores from both the experimental group and control group indicate that the experimental group gained significantly in terms of their L2 motivation. It preliminarily proves that the integrated motivational teaching model is an effective means to enhance students' L2 motivation.

4.2 Students' Self-Reports

To answer the first question, apart from the questionnaire, students' self-reports were also collected to explore the complex phenomena of L2 motivation and to help explain and validate the significant gains in the motivation questionnaire survey. In this study, the students of the experimental group were required to write self-report twice to reflect their feelings on the teaching model: after the first unit was completed and at the end of the course. Since the first one was mainly aimed to improve the researcher's teaching, for the present study, a total of 63 self-reports at the end of the semester submitted to the E-learning APP were prepared for content analysis with an inductive approach (Strauss, 1987). Based on the annotations made by the research assistants and after several times noting, color coding and commenting of the researcher, the following section will contribute to a report of students' reflection on the teaching model in terms of these three themes: (1) overall feelings over the dynamic motivational teaching model, (2) students' gains in this semester's English learning, and (3) students' favorite activities in this semester's English course.

4.2.1 Students' Overall Feelings over the Dynamic Motivational Teaching Model

Almost all students in the experimental group expressed a positive feeling about the dynamic motivational teaching model. High-frequency keywords such as "challenging", "exciting", "rich", "colorful", "friendly", "supportive", etc., can fully illustrated this point. Positive feedbacks can mainly manifest in the following two aspects.

First, students reflected this semester' English class as favorably different from their previous one. For example, Student 2 and Student 7 mentioned that:

EXCERPT 1

At the beginning, I felt that the college English was quite different from the high school and was a little nervous. The teacher paid more attention to teaching us English as a means of communication rather than a body of knowledge. Later, I slowly adapted to this way and felt that the teacher's method was very good, which fully aroused our enthusiasm. (Student 2)

EXCERPT 2

In this semester's English learning, what we focused was not only on the language forms and how it could be used in doing exercises as we did in high school, but on the real meaning and how it could be related to our life and further study. This could enhance our understanding and practical application of English, which in turn increased our interest for learning. (Student 7)

Another point many students expressed a positive difference from their previous English learning experience was the adoption of collaborative learning in this semester's English course.

EXCERPT 3

> Unlike my previous English classes, where we used to study individually and seldom communicate with classmates academically, we have done a lot of pair and group work in and out of class this semester, now I think I have become more fluent and more competent to express myself. Besides, collaboration also helps us to learn others' language and ideas during communication. (Student 23)

EXCERPT 4

> Previously in my English class in high school, my teacher always talked and students just listened. Now, I enjoyed more the collaborative activities designed by our teacher, where we group members felt freer to talk and discuss, and this motivated us to actively participate in class. (Student 39)

In addition to the POA and collaborative learning, some students noticed the salient change of this semester's English course from their high school that the researcher tried to use different teaching modes to engage them in class. For instance:

EXCERPT 5

> Different from our previous English class where what the teacher did mostly was to read the PowerPoint slides and then let us do lots of practice, in this semester, we watched many videos and

listened music, which not only made learning interesting and less boring, but also enhanced our understanding of a topic. (Student 15)

Moreover, students enjoyed a pleasant and supportive learning atmosphere created by both the teacher and their group members.

EXCERPT 6

I enjoyed the collaborative activities where we group members felt freer to talk and discuss, and this motivated us to actively participate in class. (Student 21)

EXCERPT 7

I felt more comfortable to speak English with my team members' backup. I once acted as a reporter, instead of feeling very nervous to stand up and speak in English as I used to be before, I felt quite relaxed because after a while of group talk, everyone has contributed their part and shared their idea, what I should do was to summarize and present the outcome of the team work. (Student 42)

EXCERPT 8

I had never expected the college English so engaging and stimulating is. The 3-min presentation at the beginning of class, pair work and group work, the interaction between teacher and students and even the short break between two sessions were filled with so much laughing and joking. (Student 20)

EXCERPT 9

> I want to express my gratitude to my teacher, who is so kind to us, and always smiles to us. I like the small talk before the class she has with us, which brings her closer to us. She also tends to move around when we conduct the pair and group work. Sometimes this makes me nervous to have my lame English be heard by our teacher, but I still feel happy when she joins us and sometimes gives us advice. (Student 61)

EXCERPT 10

> To me, the most motivating thing in English class is a friendly atmosphere where there is much interaction between teacher and students, I like my English teacher who always wears smile on her face, and always tells us never mind about making mistakes which is a natural part of language learning while we express ourselves. This makes us participate in the class activities more actively. (Student 3)

Some students mentioned the teacher's use of modern technology that made the English learning experience more enjoyable and fulfilling. For example,

EXCERPT 11

> The English class in this semester is quite lively and interesting. Brainstorming, Race to Answer and Voting and other activities have greatly enriched class, and enhanced the interaction between teachers and students and our enthusiasm to participate in classroom teaching activities. (Student 17)

4.2.2 The Maximum Gains After One Semester's English Learning

Despite a great variety of gains from this semester's English class students have revealed with details in their self-reports, there are some themes more distinct than the others and will be elucidated in the excerpt below. The most frequent mentioned benefits students gained were how the dynamic motivational teaching model enhanced their confidence toward learning English, especially their oral English. For example, many students mentioned that more opportunities to practice their oral English caused a breakthrough and made them more confident in opening their mouths. Students 2 described vividly the day when it was her turn to make a presentation.

© EXCERPT 12

> Thanks for the production-oriented approach, we were offered many opportunities to practice and show ourselves in English. I used to be very shy and dared not to speak in front of many people. However, seeing so many students performed so well, I was deeply encouraged and decided to make good preparations. For a couple of nights before I went on stage, I devoted myself to memorizing the draft I wrote. I was very nervous, feeling that other students would laugh at me when I spoke English with accent, but when I stood on stage and began to speak, I suddenly forgot all my concerns and worries, my focus was on what I had prepared. Finally, the applause from the students proved my success, and the teacher's positive commence increased my motivation toward learning English.

Apart from the ample opportunities to practice their English, some students reported the incredible power of group work in enabling them feel confident, expecting for the best which can finally help them produce satisfactory group work. Student 15 made her point very clear when he said, "The power of collective wisdom and role model is immense." Student 4 agreed with her by giving an account of her experience.

EXCERPT 13

> When you work together with your teammates, you can do anything. Take the video making for example, the teacher asked us to imagine we were successful person in 10 years later and were invited to make a video to her current demotivated students and tell them how English was important and how to learn well. I felt so embarrassed to speak in front of a camera, and was not willing to do, but my teammate turned to me, with her patience, help and encouragement, I finally overcame my anxiety and gathered confidence to finish that work well.

Still some students, for example, Student 49 mentioned how the teacher's positive attitude increased her confidence and overcame her anxiety in English learning.

EXCERPT 14

> I always had this idea that I was not good at in English because of my poor English pronunciation, and it kept me from being motivated and participating in class. However, when I stood in front of the other students and see Ms. Wang looking at me with an encouraging look, smile and expectation, I became even braver and more confident. After I finished, when she said, "Well done. Your voice is loud and clear, and your pronunciation is

good." I couldn't help bursting out tears. From then on, I love English even more.

Secondly, students expressed their appreciation toward this semester's English course because it taught them how to cooperate with others and helped them reap the harvest of friendship in the process of conducting collaborative learning activities.

EXCERPT 15

> Learning within a group enables us to have a better understanding about our roommates, including their interesting experiences, opinions on certain issues, etc., while discussing around a topic, we can not only complete various tasks successfully, but the interaction further strengthens the close relationship between us. (Student 24)

EXCERPT 16

> Collaborative learning allows us to make progress together in helping each other. Since the last group submitted their work, and had to give their performance to entertain the whole class during the break between two periods of class, we all felt responsible to remind and checked over each other to make sure that every group member completed his work as soon as possible. You were not working for your own interest, but for the whole group. This was fun and we learned at the same time. It improved our motivation and increased the efficiency to finish our homework. (Student 32)

The excerpt above indicated that students enjoyed collaboration, which could teach them the true value of teamwork especially when it was the time to compete with and fight against other groups. Student 23 also reflected the pride of fulfilling his group work in his self-report.

EXCERPT 17

> Our group was responsible for teaching the whole classmates the key words and expressions of Unit 2, and the quality of our work was directly depended on each group member's work and contribution. It was fun to come to the platform with my partners, which equipped me with more confidence and less anxiety. We may not have done very well, but we all tried our best. Seeing that everyone was attentive in listening to what we said, and actively answered the questions we raised, we felt that all our hard work deserved.

Another aspect students mentioned most when it came to the benefit they gained from this semester's English course was that they made noticeable improvement in their speaking ability.

EXCERPT 18

> Previously, our high school English teacher only focused on completing or covering whatever in the textbook, but the college English cared more about how we can put what we learned into use. In this semester, we did a lot of oral practice, such as the role play, pair and group discussion, debate, and a 3-min presentation at the beginning of each class, etc. Thanks to the continuous practices, I found myself make a big progress in speaking. (Student 15)

EXCERPT 19

> We have done a lot of pair and group work in and out of class this semester, now I think I have become more fluent and more competent in expressing myself. (Student 18)

4.2.3 Students' Favourite Activities in This Semester's English Class

In the self-reports, students also revealed their loved activities which they thought interesting, useful, and motivating. The following students' "experts" expressed how they enjoyed the various modes and activities in the teacher's English class.

EXCERPT 20

> I loved listening music activities and video activities which not only made learning interesting, but also enhanced our understanding of a topic. For example, when we were asked whether the modern technology changed the world always for the better, I found little to say, but after we watched a video clip from a movie *Black Mirror*, I had a clearer picture in mind to discuss both the benefits and adverse effects of modern technology, and I was also equipped with more words to say about this topic. (Student 4)

EXCERPT 21

> During the semester, we did a lot of engaging activities such as making up a role play after learning Unit 2 in the textbook, completing information gap while watching videos and trying to use them in the following writing, assessing and giving feedback

to my partner. Among these activities, the 3-min presentation of hot news at the beginning of each English class was my favourite, because the topics most of my classmates chose were always very interesting and I could learn a lot from their sharing. (Student 26)

In addition to audios and videos, many students also expressed their fond of using Superstar Learning APP, an internet online learning platform to assist English learning in and outside class.

EXCERPT 22

I find the online discussion with a topic is very engaging, where I can both air my opinion freely, and read other students' views in a relaxing environment. Besides, my publishing or replying a discussion can also help me get 5 points bonus and additional 2 points bonus if I get the teacher's praise for this course regular assessment. I find it very motivating. (Student 39)

Meanwhile some students spoke highly of collaborative learning and the activities when learning together with their classmates.

EXCERPT 23

For instance, the Adapted Jigsaw Reading, where I needed to learn together with my friends and teach other students. During the vocabulary quiz, we had to prepare different PowerPoint slides with the new words learnt form them, then we had other groups to guess the word or expression on the slide through their cooperation. It's funny! (Student 23)

EXCERPT 24

> I found the STAD was very exciting. I always paid attention to every opportunity that I might earn some points for our group. My English was not very good, but I still tried to give answers when a question was raised by my teacher. Whenever I earned some scores for my group, I felt good about myself. (Student 17)

Still there were students who enjoyed the teacher's promoting the English-related values and activities that can encourage them to communicate in English.

EXCERPT 25

> I like to listen to my English teacher speak in English, though sometimes I can't understand all of what she has said. I was drawn whenever she told us her experience of going abroad and her overseas study, especially the cross-cultural communication and how she used English to cope with things in life and study and accustomed to the new environment. This not only opens a window to gain an insight to the outside world but also let us know how English is important if I want to travel or study abroad. (Student 25)

EXCERPT 26

> I think the English corner organized by our teacher every Friday evening in the library is marvellous for us to practice our English. To be honest, oral English has always been my weak point, maybe because I start English late compared to other urban area students, so I feel quite inferior and dare not to open my mouth, but the English corner provides us atmosphere to

express ourselves. I still remember one day when I talked with an overseas exchange student from Australia, though during our exchange there were some problems, and I did not know how to express myself, we still talked long and laughed happily, during which I knew a lot of amazing things from his country. (Student 21)

Another common favorite activity students mentioned was L2 ideal self activity which they considered it very helpful in increasing their motivation in learning English.

EXCERPT 27

Luckily, our college English teacher has attached great importance to our goal set and attainment of English learning. Under her guide of possible self, my dream about English is not merely passing the examination, but also becoming an HR in an international company who are equipped with the opportunity to be designated by the company to work or study abroad because of my excellent English. I know it is not easy, so I determine to study hard and carry out my action plan conscientiously to the full. (Student 15)

From the quotation above, we can see that for Student 15, her life dream is related to English (to become a HR at an international company), besides, she knows she needs to fulfill her dream by hard work. Considering this, it is no wonder that she has made a remarkable progress in the post English proficiency test compared to her pre-test score.

Students' self-reports showed that by applying the dynamic motivational teaching model, the researcher designed many engaging lessons that incorporated a great variety of production tasks, collaborative activities, modern technologic means and motivational strategies, to actively involve students in the learning process, which ultimately increased students' motivated learning behaviors.

To sum up, both the quantitative and qualitative data as well as the self-reported data serve as reported in this part indicate that this integrated motivational teaching model combined by the four motivating components is effective in enhancing motivation to learn English in the Chinese college English context.

To examine the effects of the motivational teaching on English learning, in this section, the results of the oral test and the written test as well as each of the four items in the written test (writing, listening, reading and translation) are reported to examine the effects of the motivational teaching on the EFL learners' language proficiency gains.

4.3 The Result of Proficiency Tests

4.3.1 The Results of the Oral Test

For the measurement of the participants' overall language proficiency, both the experimental group and the control group took the oral and written test twice, one as the pre-test, and the other as the post-test in the whole process of experimental teaching. First, the analysis of the oral test before and after the treatment was made on the experimental group. As indicated in Table 4.8, the mean score of the post-oral test was 4.643, and compared with 3.548 they got from the pre-test, such gain was statistically significant since the p-value was as low as 0.000. By contrast, the mean score of the post oral performance in the control group was 3.798, only slightly higher than 3.607 in the pre-test, therefore the difference between the two tests was not statistically significant, in other words, the control group did not make as significant improvement as the experimental group in the oral performance.

Table 4.8 Intra-Group Statistics of Pre- and Post-Oral Test (*N* of Each Group=42)

Item	Groups	Time	Mean	SD	*t*-value	*p*-value
Oral test	Experimental	Pre	3.548	1.119	-7.838	0.000 ***
		Post	4.643	0.878		
	Control	Pre	3.607	0.815	-1.864	0.069
		Post	3.798	0.698		

In addition to the intra-group comparison analysis presented above, the results of the inter-group analysis were also reported on the oral test. As is shown in Table 4.9, both groups obtained almost the same score on the pre-test with the mean score of the control group 3.607, and 3.584 for the experimental group. Therefore, there was no significant difference between the two groups in the pre-test. However, after one semester's motivational teaching treatment, the score of the oral test in the experimental group (*M*=4.643) was much higher than that in the control group (*M*=3.798). As displayed in Table 4.9, a significant difference of the two groups in their post-test was obtained since the *p*-value was as low as 0.000, indicating that the students in the experimental group made greater progress in their oral English than students in the control group.

Table 4.9 Inter-Group Statistics of Pre- and Post-Test Oral Test (*N* of Each Group=42)

Item	Time	Groups	Mean	SD	*t*-value	*p*-value
Oral test	Pre	Experimental	3.548	1.119	-0.278	0.781
		Control	3.607	0.815		
	Post	Experimental	4.643	0.878	4.879	0.000 ***
		Control	3.798	0.698		

4.3.2 The Results of the Written Test

In terms of the written test, as illustrated in Table 4.10, a significant difference between pre- and post-test can be found in both groups, with the p-value of the experimental group being 0.000 and 0.001 for the control group, that is to say, both groups made significant progress in their post-written test compared to their pre-written test, but the improvement degree was different in favour of the experimental group, as the experimental group developed their proficiency from the mean score of 47.321 in the pre-test to 55.333 in the post-test while the control group developed from the mean score of 47.750 to 52.369. In other words, though students in both groups improved significantly in their English written performance, they treated by the motivational teaching model still outperformed the students in the regular college English class for their more dramatic academic gains.

Table 4.10 Intra-Group Statistics of Pre- and Post-Written Test (N of Each Group=42)

Item	Groups	Time	Mean	SD	t-value	p-value
Written test	Experimental	Pre	47.321	10.820	-5.027	0.000 ***
		Post	55.333	11.453		
	Control	Pre	47.750	12.126	-3.491	0.001 **
		Post	52.369	11.308		

After the within-group comparison, let's turn to the results of the inter-group analysis of the written test. From Table 4.11, we can see that with the p-value of 0.865, there was not significant difference between the two groups in their pre-test, likewise, no significant difference was found in the post-test either, though the mean of the experimental group was 2.96 point higher than that of the control group, that is to say, both the experimental group and control group have made improvement after one semester's English learning.

Table 4.11 Inter-Group Statistics of Pre- and Post-Test Written Task (*N* of Each Group=42)

Item	Time	Groups	Mean	*SD*	*t*-value	*p*-value
Written test	Pre	Experimental	47.321	10.820	-0.171	0.865
		Control	47.750	12.126		
	Post	Experimental	55.333	11.453	1.194	0.236
		Control	52.369	11.308		

4.3.3 The Results of Four Language Skills in the Written Test

In addition to comparing the total score of the written test between the two groups, the intra- and inter-group analysis of the four items—writing, listening, reading and translation involving in the written test were also investigated for further analysis. Firstly, the comparison of the four items on the intra-group difference was made in the experimental group as shown in Table 4.12.

Table 4.12 Paired Samples Test of Four Skills in Written Test on the Intra-Group of Experimental Group (*N*=42)

Items	Groups	Time	Mean	*SD*	*t*-value	*p*-value
Listening	Experimental	Pre	15.667	4.594	-2.646	0.011 *
		Post	17.786	5.702		
Reading	Experimental	Pre	13.869	5.639	-2.148	0.038 *
		Post	16.124	4.539		
Translation	Experimental	Pre	7.976	3.645	-2.737	0.009 **
		Post	9.905	3.856		
Composition	Experimental	Pre	9.714	2.200	-6.511	0.000 ***
		Post	11.357	1.679		

As illustrated in Table 4.12, the experimental group gained a significant progress in all of the four skills in the written test, among which listening and reading demonstrated a significant difference with the p-values lower than 0.05, and translation showed quite a significant difference ($p=0.009<0.01$), while composition saw the extreme significant difference ($p=0.000<0.001$). That is to say, the experimental group improved in all of the four skills in the written test. Specifically, composition showed the most remarkable progress, and the second great improvement belonged to translation followed by listening, while reading made the least progress.

By contrast, instead of making significant gains in all of the four skills like the experimental group, the control group, as indicated in Table 4.13, gained significantly only on the skill of reading. The mean score of the pre-test was 14.345 while that of the post-test was 17.095 with the p-value of 0.006. Except that, the other three skills—listening, translation and composition did not find any sign of significant progress on the post-test.

Table 4.13   Paired Samples Test of Four Items in Written Test on the Intra-Group of Control Group ($N=42$)

Items	Group	Time	Mean	SD	t-value	p-value
Listening	Control	Pre	15.952	5.508	-0.142	0.888
		Post	16.048	4.873		
Reading	Control	Pre	14.345	6.165	-2.920	0.006 **
		Post	17.095	5.195		
Translation	Control	Pre	7.667	2.816	-1.966	0.056
		Post	8.690	4.087		
Composition	Control	Pre	9.833	1.962	0.157	0.876
		Post	9.786	2.006		

After the intra-group comparison, the next section examined the inter-group difference in the four items in the written test using the Independent Sample Test. The first analysis comes to the listening part. According to Table 4.14, though the control group got a slightly higher score than the experimental group with the mean difference of 0.29 in the pre-test, the experimental group scored 1.74 points higher than the experimental group in the post-test. But both of the two differences were not significant ($p=0.797$ in the pre-test and $p=0.137$ in the post-test). For reading part, both the pre- and post-test saw that the control group scored slightly higher than the experimental group, but the difference was not significant either ($p=0.713$ in the pre-test and $p=0.364$ in the post test). That is to say, both the experimental group and the control group made improvement in listening, reading, but there was no significant difference between the two groups in the pre-test and post-test. In other words, the experimental group achieved as well as the control group in the two language skills. However, things were quite different in composition and translation. The result of the pre-test in composition and translation showed that there was no significant difference between the two groups, in other words, the experimental group and the control group were at a similar level in terms of the two skills when the experimental study began, but the experimental group outperformed the control group significantly in the post-test. The mean score of the post translation task in the experimental group was 10.786, while that of the control group was 8.690, and the mean difference of the 2.096 was statistically significant ($p=0.005<0.05$). The same situation can be seen in the composition part, but with even more noticeable significant difference in the post-test between the two groups as the p-value was as low as 0.00. (See Table 4.14 for details.)

Table 4.14   Independent Samples Test of Four Items in Written Test (*N* of Each Group=42)

Items	Tests	Groups	Mean	*SD*	*t*-value	*p*-value
Listening	Pre	Experimental	15.667	4.594	-0.258	0.797
		Control	15.952	5.508		
	Post	Experimental	17.786	5.702	1.502	0.137
		Control	16.048	4.873		
Reading	Pre	Experimental	13.869	5.639	-0.369	0.713
		Control	14.345	6.165		
	Post	Experimental	16.124	4.539	-0.912	0.364
		Control	17.095	5.195		
Translation	Pre	Experimental	7.976	3.645	0.435	0.664
		Control	7.667	2.816		
	Post	Experimental	10.786	2.279	2.901	0.005 **
		Control	8.690	4.087		
Composition	Pre	Experimental	9.714	2.200	-0.262	0.794
		Control	9.833	1.962		
	Post	Experimental	11.357	1.679	3.892	0.000 ***
		Control	9.786	2.006		

4.3.4 The Summary of the Comparison Between the Two Groups

In sum, as shown in Table 4.15, the results of the intra-group comparisons of the oral and written test between the pre-and post-test revealed that the experimental made a significant progress in all of the five language skills, while the control group gained significantly only in reading. The results of the inter-group comparison as found in Table 4.16 demonstrated that the experimental group achieved as well as the control group in the receptive knowledge (reading, listening), but the former was far superior to the letter in the productive knowledge (translation, composition) after one semester's motivational teaching treatment. Therefore, it proves the effect of the motivational teaching model in improving the L2 learners' English proficiency.

Table 4.15 The Intra-Group Comparison of the Experimental Group and Control Group

		Experimental group (*N*=42)					Control group (*N*=42)				
Skills	Tests	Mean	SD	Percent improvement	*t*-value	*p*-value	Mean	SD	Percent improvement	*t*-value	*p*-value
Speaking	Pre	3.548	1.119	30.9%	-7.838	0.000 ***	3.607	0.815	5.3%	-1.864	0.096
	Post	4.463	0.878				3.798	0.698			
Listening	Pre	15.667	4.594	13.5%	-2.646	0.011 *	15.952	5.508	0.6%	-0.142	0.888
	Post	17.786	5.702				16.048	4.873			
Reading	Pre	13.869	5.639	16.3%	-2.148	0.038 *	14.345	6.165	19.2%	-2.920	0.006 **
	Post	16.124	4.539				17.095	5.195			
Translation	Pre	7.976	3.645	24.2%	-2.737	0.009 **	7.667	2.816	13.3%	-1.966	0.056
	Post	9.905	3.856				8.690	4.087			
Composition	Pre	9.714	2.200	16.9%	-6.511	0.000 ***	9.833	1.962	-0.5%	0.157	0.876
	Post	11.357	1.679				9.786	2.006			

Table 4.16 The Inter-Group Comparison Between the Experimental Group and Control Group

Skills	Groups	Pre-test				Post-test			
		Mean	SD	*t*-value	*p*-value	Mean	SD	*t*-value	*p*-value
Speaking	Experimental	3.548	1.119	-0.278	0.781	4.643	0.878	4.879	0.000 ***
	Control	3.607	0.815			3.798	0.698		
Listening	Experimental	15.667	4.594	-0.369	0.713	17.786	5.702	1.502	0.137
	Control	15.952	5.508			16.048	4.873		
Reading	Experimental	13.869	5.639	-2.148	0.038 *	16.124	4.539	-0.912	0.364
	Control	14.345	6.165			17.095	5.195		
Translation	Experimental	7.976	3.654	-2.737	0.009 **	9.905	3.856	2.901	0.005 **
	Control	7.667	2.816			8.690	4.087		
Composition	Experimental	9.714	2.200	-6.511	0.000 ***	11.357	1.679	3.892	0.000 ***
	Control	9.833	1.962			9.786	2.006		

4.4 Effects of Motivational Teaching Model on High/ Medium/Low Achievers

As mentioned in the research design in Chapter 3, for the sake of operation and confidence of the oral test, 72 students of the experimental class and 71 students of the control class were divided into three subgroups based on their English scores in the entrance examination, from which 14 students of each subgroup, altogether 42 participants from each class were randomly selected for further study. This section presents a further study on the effect of the motivational teaching on the three subgroups of different levels of English proficiency in both groups.

4.4.1 Results of the Oral Test

In order to investigate the intra-group differences in the students' oral performance, Paired Samples Test was adopted to compare the scores of the oral test of three subgroups in both the experimental and control group.

4.4.1.1 The Comparison of the Oral Test Scores in the Experimental Group

The first comparison was made on the high-achievers in the experimental group. It has been found in Table 4.17, all of the three subgroups of high, medium and low achievers improved significantly in the post-test oral examination, among which the low-achievers made the biggest progress with the mean of 4.250 in the post-test against 3.000 in the pre-test, the 1.25 mean difference was statistically significant as the p-value was 0.000. The same significant p-value ($p=0.000$) can also be seen in the medium achievers, indicating that the statistical difference between the pre- and post-test was significant, though the mean difference of 1.214 between the two tests was slightly lower comparing to the low-achievers. Finally, in spite of the highest mean score gained by the high-achievers in the post-test ($M=4.964$), this subgroup experienced the comparatively smaller mean difference between the two tests with the *p*-value of 0.002.

Table 4.17 Paired Samples Statistics of Three Subgroups in Experimental Group in Oral Test (*N* of Each Group=14)

Subgroups	Tests	Mean	*SD*	*t*-value	*p*-value
H-group	Pre	4.143	0.949	-3.846	0.002 **
	Post	4.964	0.771		
M-group	Pre	3.500	1.037	-4.757	0.000 ***
	Post	4.714	0.726		
L-group	Pre	3.000	1.126	-4.894	0.000 ***
	Post	4.250	1.014		

4.4.1.2 The Comparison of the Oral Test Scores in the Control Group

As a sharp contrast, it was found in Table 4.18 that no significant difference was identified in any of the subgroups, as the *p*-values of three subgroups in the two tests were all higher than 0.5. The biggest mean difference between the two tests was 0.215 gained by the low-achievers, but it was much lower than that in the experimental group.

Table 4.18 Paired Samples Statistics of Three Subgroups in Control Group in Oral Test (*N* of Each Group =14)

Subgroups	Tests	Mean	*SD*	*t*-value	*p*-value
H-group	Pre	3.679	0.846	-0.891	0.389
	Post	3.857	0.534		
M-group	Pre	4.071	0.675	-1.046	0.315
	Post	4.250	0.612		
L-group	Pre	3.071	0.615	-1.249	0.234
	Post	3.286	0.611		

4.4.1.3 The Comparison of Pre-Test Scores from the Experimental and Control Group

From the two tables above, we can see that the all of the three subgroups in the experimental group made a significant progress in their oral performance during the experimental period while none of the three subgroups in the control group showed any significant growth on their spoken English under the traditional teaching model.

After comparing scores of the oral tests within the subgroups, the Independent Sample Test was computed to examine the inter-group improvement on students' speaking competence.

It can be seen from Table 4.19 that the high achievers in the experimental group scored a little higher than their counterparts in the control group in the pre-test. The mean score of this subgroup in the experimental group was 4.143 against 3.679 gained by the control group in the pre-test. The situation was reversed in terms of the medium group, as this subgroup in the control group scored a little higher than that in the experimental group, with the mean difference of 4.071 in the control against 3.500 in the experimental group. For the low group, the score for this subgroup in each group was almost the same with $M=3.000$ for the experimental group and $M=3.071$ for the control group. But no significant difference was found in any of the three subgroups in the pre-test. In other words, the three subgroups in both the experimental and control group were in the similar level of their oral English before the experimental teaching started.

Table 4.19 Independent Samples Statistics of Subgroups in Pre-Oral Test (*N* of Each Group=14)

Subgroups	Groups	Mean	SD	t-value	p-value
H-group	Experimental	4.143	0.949	1.366	0.184
	Control	3.679	0.846		
M-group	Experimental	3.500	1.037	-1.727	0.096
	Control	4.071	0.675		
L-group	Experimental	3.000	1.126	-0.208	0.837
	Control	3.071	0.615		

4.4.1.4 The Comparison of Post-Test Scores from the Experimental and Control Group

The following section will see the examination of the post-test data. As illustrated in Table 4.20, both the high and low achievers in the experimental group outperformed significantly than their counterparts in the control group in the post-test oral performance. The mean score of high achievers in the experimental group increased to 4.964, comparing to 3.857 of the control group, the mean difference between the two high subgroups in the post-test oral performance was as high as 1.107 and was statistically significant ($p=0.00$). Likewise, with the mean score of 4.250 for the low achievers in the experimental group against 3.826 in the control group, the difference was also of statistical significance ($p=0.005$). Although without statistical difference for the medium achievers ($p=0.79$), the fact that this subgroup in the experimental group gained the mean score of 0.464 more than the control group on the post oral test was also impressive.

Table 4.20 Independent Samples Statistics of Subgroups in Post-Oral Test (*N* of Each Group=14)

Subgroups	Groups	Mean	*SD*	*t*-value	*p*-value
H-group	Experimental	4.964	0.771	4.415	0.000 ***
	Control	3.857	0.534		
M-group	Experimental	4.714	0.726	1.829	0.079
	Control	4.250	0.612		
L-group	Experimental	4.250	1.014	3.047	0.005 **
	Control	3.286	0.611		

4.4.2 Results of the Written Test

In order to investigate the difference in the students' written test within and between subgroups, the total written scores as well as the score of each language skill—listening, reading, translation and composition covered in the written test would all undergo careful examinations.

4.4.2.1 The Comparison of the Written Test Scores in the Experimental Group

The first comparison fell on the intra-group improvement using the Paired Samples Test. The results presented in Table 4.21 revealed the total written score of each subgroup of the experimental group. It can be seen that the high (p=0.02) and low achievers (p=0.03) made a significant progress after one semester's motivational intervention while the medium achievers (p=0.60) did not show any significant growth on their written performance during the experimental period. To be specific, the low-achievers made the most remarkable progress while the high achievers took the second place in developing their English proficiency as shown in Table 4.21, and the low achievers scored 9.643 in their post-test more than that in pre-test while the high achievers achieved the mean difference of 9.392 between the two tests. However, with the mean difference of 3.286, the medium group showed only limited progress in their levels of English proficiency but without statistical significance.

Table 4.21 Paired Samples Statistics of Written Test of Subgroups in Experimental Group (*N* of Each Group=14)

Subgroups	Tests	Mean	SD	*t*-value	*p*-value
H-group	Pre	54.679	10.321	-3.948	0.002 **
	Post	64.071	9.252		
M-group	Pre	49.321	6.979	-0.058	0.060
	Post	52.607	8.463		
L-group	Pre	40.036	8.659	-3.596	0.003 **
	Post	49.679	8.066		

4.4.2.2 The Comparison of the Written Test Scores in the Control Group

Then, let's turn to the control group. The same significant improvement can also be found in the low achievers in the post test as shown in Table 4.22. The score of the post-test was 45.964 as opposed to 38.429 in the pre-test, and the *p*-value was 0.009. But except for this subgroup, the high and medium achievers did not show any sign of significant improvement on the written post-test.

Table 4.22   Paired Samples Written Statistics of Subgroups in Control Group (*N* of Each Group=14)

Subgroups	Tests	Mean	SD	*t*-value	*p*-value
H-group	Pre	47.250	8.502	-1.215	0.246
	Post	53.893	10.044		
M-group	Pre	55.500	11.490	-1.215	0.246
	Post	58.536	12.742		
L-group	Pre	38.429	11.050	-3.073	0.009 **
	Post	45.964	9.174		

4.4.3 The Comparison of the Four Language Skills Between the Experimental and Control Group

To make a further analysis, the examination of the scores of the four language skills involved in the written test was also made to each of the subgroups in the two groups prior to and after the teaching experiment. The results of the pre-test and post-test of each language skill are illustrated in Table 4.23.

4.4.3.1 The Comparison of the Four Language Skills of High Achievers

It can be seen from Table 4.23 that high-achievers in the experimental group gained significantly in the written post-test on all of the four language skills. In other words, the high-achievers in the experimental group made a statistically significant progress on listening, reading, translation and composition. As a sharp contrast, no significant difference can be found in high-achievers on all of the four language skills between the two tests. In other words, the high-achievers in the control group did not make any statistically significant improvement on listening, reading, translation and composition.

Table 4.23 Paired Samples Test of Each Language Skill in Written Test of High Achievers (*N* of Each Group=14)

Items	Groups	Tests	Mean	SD	*t*-value	*p*-value
Listening	Experimental	Pre	18.857	4.504	-2.482	0.028 *
		Post	22.286	4.858		
	Control	Pre	20.429	4.925	1.764	0.101
		Post	18.357	5.799		
Reading	Experimental	Pre	15.750	5.094	-2.453	0.029 *
		Post	18.857	3.146		
	Control	Pre	15.786	6.320	-1.705	0.112
		Post	19.214	5.966		
Translation	Experimental	Pre	9.429	2.533	-3.879	0.002 **
		Post	11.786	1.761		
	Control	Pre	9.571	2.101	-0.392	0.702
		Post	9.857	3.301		
Composition	Experimental	Pre	10.214	2.190	-3.702	0.003 **
		Post	12.000	1.467		
	Control	Pre	10.357	1.446	0.000	1.000
		Post	10.357	2.205		

4.4.3.2 The Comparison of the Four Language Skills of Medium Achievers

Next was on the medium subgroup. Table 4.24 revealed that the experimental group made a significant advance on translation ($p=0.19$) and composition ($p=0.00$) but not on listening and reading. When it comes to the control group, no significant improvement can be found in this subgroup on any of the four language skills, what's worse, in contrast to the significant progress made by the medium achievers on composition in the experimental group, the score of this subgroup in the control group even decreased significantly in the post-test as shown in Table 4.24. The medium-achievers in the control group scored 10.643 in the pre-test, but dropped to 9.429 in the post-test. The mean difference between the two tests was a statistically significant fall as the *p*-value was as low as 0.032<0.05.

Table 4.24   Paired Samples Test of Each Language Skill in Written Test of Medium Achievers (*N* of Each Group=14)

Items	Groups	Tests	Mean	SD	*t*-value	*p*-value
Listening	Experimental	Pre	14.143	3.570	-1.233	0.239
		Post	16.071	4.827		
	Control	Pre	15.286	3.268	-0.302	0.767
		Post	15.571	4.397		
Reading	Experimental	Pre	14.893	6.029	-0.483	0.637
		Post	15.893	4.156		
	Control	Pre	15.607	4.919	-1.919	0.077
		Post	17.964	4.592		
Translation	Experimental	Pre	8.786	3.468	-2.670	0.019 *
		Post	10.714	2.127		
	Control	Pre	7.714	3.049	-1.220	0.244
		Post	8.929	4.141		
Composition	Experimental	Pre	9.571	2.408	-5.140	0.000 ***
		Post	11.071	1.979		
	Control	Pre	10.643	1.392	2.406	0.032 *
		Post	9.429	2.376		

4.4.3.3 The Comparison of the Four Language Skills of Low Achievers

As to the low achievers, it was found in Table 4.25 that a significant progress in the experimental group can be seen, just like the medium achievers, on translation (*p*=0.05) and composition (*p*=0.00) while the other two language skills, listening and reading did not show any sign of improvement (*p*>0.1). But for the control group, similar to the high achievers, no significant improvement can be found in the low achievers on any of the four language skills.

Table 4.25 Paired Samples Test of Each Language Skill in Written Test of Low Achievers (*N* of Each Group=14)

Items	Groups	Tests	Mean	*SD*	*t*-value	*p*-value
Listening	Experimental	Pre	14.000	4.132	-0.821	0.426
		Post	15.000	4.723		
	Control	Pre	12.143	4.801	-1.800	0.095
		Post	14.214	3.512		
Reading	Experimental	Pre	10.964	4.896	-1.274	0.225
		Post	13.621	4.793		
	Control	Pre	11.643	6.628	-1.477	0.164
		Post	14.107	3.627		
Translation	Experimental	Pre	5.714	3.871	-3.418	0.005 **
		Post	9.571	2.622		
	Control	Pre	5.714	1.815	-1.592	0.136
		Post	7.286	4.581		
Composition	Experimental	Pre	9.357	2.060	-4.894	0.000 ***
		Post	11.000	1.467		
	Control	Pre	8.500	2.278	-2.025	0.064
		Post	9.571	1.283		

After comparing the intra-group improvement of the high, medium and low achievers on the total scores as well as each item of the written pre- and post-tests, the next section will examine the inter-group difference in the pre- and post-written test.

4.4.3.4 The Comparison of the Overall Scores of the Experimental and Control Group

The first comparison was on the overall score of the written test. The result in Table 4.26 showed that all of the subgroups in both the experimental and control group made progress, but in different degrees. The high achievers in the experimental group scored 5.535 more than the control group did in the post-test, and the mean score of low achievers was 3.715 higher than that of the control group. The slight mean difference can be seen in medium achievers between both groups with mere 1.286 in favour of the experimental group. But there was no significant difference between any of the subgroups in the two groups in both the pre-test and post-test. In other words, all of the three subgroups in the experimental group outperformed their counterpart in the control group in the overall written score, but did not make a statistically significant difference.

Table 4.26 Independent Samples Tests of Subgroups in Written Test (N of Each Group=14)

Subgroups	Tests	Groups	Mean	SD	t-value	p-value
H-group	Pre	Experimental	54.679	10.321	-0.199	0.844
		Control	55.500	11.490		
	Post	Experimental	64.071	9.252	1.315	0.200
		Control	58.536	12.742		
M-group	Pre	Experimental	47.250	8.502	-0.705	0.487
		Control	49.321	6.979		
	Post	Experimental	53.893	10.044	0.366	0.717
		Control	52.607	8.463		
L-group	Pre	Experimental	40.036	8.659	0.428	0.672
		Control	38.429	11.053		
	Post	Experimental	49.679	8.066	1.138	0.266
		Control	45.964	9.174		

4.4.4 The Comparison of Scores of Different Skills from High Achievers

In the following part, each item covered in the written test was to be examined among the three subgroups to get a better understanding of the difference between groups. Firstly, the analysis was made on the high achievers. According to Table 4.27, of all the four language skills, that is, listening, reading, translation and composition, there was only one item (composition) that displayed a statistical significance in the post-test between the high achievers of the two groups. The mean score of composition of the high achievers in the experimental group was 12.000 against 10.357 of the score gained by the control subgroup. With the mean difference of 1.643 in the favour of the experimental subgroup, and the *p*-value of 0.028<0.05, it was safely to say that the high achievers in the experimental group were superior to their counterparts in this language skill development. The other three items did not demonstrate any significant difference between the high achievers in the two groups.

Table 4.27 Independent Samples Test of Each Language Skill in Written Test of High Achievers (*N* of Each Group=14)

Item	Time	Group	Mean	SD	*t*-value	*p*-value
Listening	Pre	Experimental	18.857	4.504	-0.881	0.386
		Control	20.429	4.925		
	Post	Experimental	22.286	4.858	1.943	0.063
		Control	18.357	5.799		
Reading	Pre	Experimental	15.750	5.094	-0.016	0.987
		Control	15.786	6.320		
	Post	Experimental	18.857	3.146	-0.198	0.845
		Control	19.214	5.966		
Translation	Pre	Experimental	9.429	2.533	-0.162	0.872
		Control	9.571	2.101		
	Post	Experimental	11.786	1.761	1.928	0.065
		Control	9.857	3.301		
Composition	Pre	Experimental	10.214	2.190	-0.204	0.840
		Control	10.357	1.446		
	Post	Experimental	12.000	1.467	2.321	0.028 *
		Control	10.357	2.205		

4.4.4.1 The Comparison of Scores of Different Skills from the Medium Achievers

Likewise, the scores of each item for the medium achievers in both groups were also computed using the Independent Samples Test to compare the inter-group differences of the medium-achievers' language skill development in both groups, as shown in Table 4.28, except for the composition where the control group experienced a slight drop in the post-test compared to the prior one, the other three items showed that both subgroups made certain progress in listening, reading and translation. The biggest mean difference existed in reading, then followed by composition, translation and listening in order, all in favour of the experimental group. But no significant difference was found in any item involved in the written test, that is to say, the medium achievers in both groups developed their language competence at the similar level, and this subgroup in the control group did not achieve significantly better than those in the experimental group.

Table 4.28   Independent Samples Test of Each Language Skill in Written Test of Medium Achievers (N of Each Group=14)

Items	Tests	Groups	Mean	SD	t-value	p-value
Listening	Pre	Experimental	14.143	3.570	-0.883	0.385
		Control	15.286	3.268		
	Post	Experimental	16.071	4.827	0.286	0.777
		Control	15.571	4.397		
Reading	Pre	Experimental	14.893	6.029	-0.343	0.734
		Control	15.607	4.919		
	Post	Experimental	15.893	4.156	-1.251	0.222
		Control	17.964	4.592		
Translation	Pre	Experimental	8.786	3.468	0.868	0.393
		Control	7.714	3.049		
	Post	Experimental	10.714	2.127	1.435	0.163
		Control	8.929	4.141		
Composition	Pre	Experimental	9.571	2.408	-1.441	0.162
		Control	10.643	1.392		
	Post	Experimental	11.071	1.979	1.987	0.057
		Control	9.429	2.376		

4.4.4.2 The Comparison of Scores of Different Skills from Low Achievers

Finally, the data comparison went to the low achievers. As shown in Table 4.29, just as was the situation in the high achievers, there was only one item-composition that demonstrated the significant difference between the two subgroups. The mean score of the experimental group was 11.000, which was 1.429 higher than that of the control group, and the p-value was as low as 0.011, indicating that the low achievers in the experimental group made a significant improvement than those in the control group. Other than that, no significant difference can be found in listening, reading and translation.

Table 4.29 Independent Samples Test of Each Language Skill in Written Test of Low Achievers (N of Each Group=14)

Items	Tests	Groups	Mean	SD	t-value	p-value
Listening	Pre	Experimental	14.000	4.132	1.097	0.283
		Control	12.143	4.801		
	Post	Experimental	15.000	4.723	0.499	0.622
		Control	14.214	3.512		
Reading	Pre	Experimental	10.964	4.896	-0.308	0.760
		Control	11.643	6.628		
	Post	Experimental	13.621	4.793	-0.302	0.765
		Control	14.107	3.627		
Translation	Pre	Experimental	5.714	3.871	0.000	1.000
		Control	5.714	1.815		
	Post	Experimental	9.571	2.622	1.620	0.117
		Control	7.286	4.581		
Composition	Pre	Experimental	9.357	2.060	1.044	0.306
		Control	8.500	2.278		
	Post	Experimental	11.000	1.467	2.741	0.011 *
		Control	9.571	1.283		

4.4.5 The Summary of the Comparison Between the Three Subgroups of the Two Groups

To sum up, the high achievers in the experimental group gained significantly both in their oral and total written performance, including all the language skills (listening, treading, translation and composition) covered in the written test in the intra-group analysis, while this subgroup in the control group did not make any significant progress in both tests. The high achievers in the experimental group also scored significantly higher in oral performance and composition in the written test than their counterparts in the control group in the inter-group analysis. The medium achievers in the experimental group advanced significantly in their oral performance, translation and composition in the written test compared with the pre-test, while this subgroup in the control group did not make any significant progress in these areas. But no significant difference can be found in the intra-group analysis of either oral or written test in the medium achievers between the two groups. For the low achievers, those in the experimental group improved significantly in both the oral and overall written performance, as well as translation and composition in the written test, while those in the control group only made a significant progress in the total written score with no significant difference can be found in any item covered in this test. The low achievers in the experimental group also gained significantly more in the inter-group analysis of oral, translation and composition performance. Such results suggested that the motivational teaching model was effective for the high achievers in improving their overall English proficiency, and for medium- and low-achievers in enhancing their oral communicative competence and writing ability. The traditional teaching model was effective, only displayed on the written test score of the low achievers.

4.5 Summary

The main purpose of this research was to examine the effectiveness of the dynamic motivational teaching model in the Chinese college English context.

4.5.1 Integration of the Findings from Quantitative and Qualitative Studies

In this chapter, both the quantitative and the qualitative findings were reported to answer the research questions on:

Q1. What are the effects of the dynamic motivational English teaching model on the EFL learners' motivation toward learning English as a foreign language?

Q2. What are the effects of the dynamic motivational English teaching model on the improvement of the EFL learners' English proficiency?

Q3. What are the effects of the dynamic motivational English teaching model on the high/medium/low English academic achievers in a heterogeneous class?

To answer these questions, finally the quantitative results and qualitative findings were integrated as a foundation of analysis. Table 4.30 presents the mains findings derived from both the quantitative and qualitative studies.

Table 4.30 Integration of Quantitative and Qualitative Findings

Determined themes of effectiveness	Quantitative		Qualitative	
	Question	Result	Question	Result
L2 learning motivation	Q1	The experimental group perceived a higher motivation.	Q1	Students reported positive opinions.
Improvement of the learners' English proficiency	Q2	The experimental group improved significantly.	–	–
Students of different English levels	Q3	High/medium/low group improved significantly.	–	–

4.5.2 Summary on the Improvement of Students' Motivation

Quantitative results indicated that the experimental group gained significantly in terms of motivational change toward learning English before and after the study, as a sharp contrast, there was a significant drop of the motivational intensity in the control group. The learners under the dynamic motivational teaching model were more highly motivated in learning English as a foreign language compared with those in the control group. They tended to have more positive attitude toward this course, more confidence in learning and using English in and outside class, more enhanced ideal second language self and less anxiety in learning English compared to students in the control group. The students' self-reports in the experimental group also confirmed the results. Most students reflected this semester's English class as favourably different from their previous one, and they described that the English course was challenging and exciting, the learning materials rich and colourful, the learning atmosphere friendly and relaxing, and the English teacher very enthusiastic, supportive and devoted. They developed their interest and confidence in English as they learnt and practiced this foreign language, and got help and support from each other.

4.5.3 Summary on the Improvement of Students' English Proficiency

The experimental group made a significant improvement on their overall English proficiency in their post-test when comparing with their pre-test score, however, counterparts in the control group only gained significantly in reading in the intra-group comparison. The inter-group comparison showed that the language skills of speaking, translation and composition of the learners in the experimental group were superior to those in the control group. With regard to the listening and reading, the experimental group scored higher than their counterparts, but no significant difference was found between these two groups of learners. (See Table 4.31 for details.)

Table 4.31 The Comparison Between the Post-Test of the Experimental Group and Control Group (*N* of Each Group=42)

Proficiency results	Group	Mean	*SD*	*t*-value	*p*-value
Oral test (Full score=9)	Experimental	4.643	0.878	4.879	0.000 ***
	Control	3.798	0.698		
Written test (Full score=100)	Experimental	53.333	11.453	1.194	0.236
	Control	52.369	11.308		
Listening (Full score=35)	Experimental	17.786	5.702	1.502	0.137
	Control	16.048	4.873		
Reading (Full score=35)	Experimental	16.124	4.539	-0.912	0.364
	Control	17.095	5.195		
Translation (Full score=15)	Experimental	10.786	2.279	2.901	0.005 **
	Control	8.690	4.087		
Composition (Full score=15)	Experimental	11.357	1.679	3.892	0.000 ***
	Control	9.786	2.006		

4.5.4 Summary on the Improvement of Students with Different Levels of English Proficiency

In addition to the whole-group comparisons, the effects of the motivational teaching model for learners with different initial levels of English achievement were also investigated. The results showed that the high achievers in the experimental group made a significant improvement on their overall English proficiency in comparison with their counterparts in the control group, and outperformed those in the control group in speaking and writing. The medium achievers improved significantly on their speaking, translation and writing compared with their counterparts in the control group, and performed as well as those in the control group in the overall proficiency. The low achievers progressed significantly in speaking, translation and writing in comparison with their counterparts in the control group and performed better in speaking and composition than those in the control group.

Chapter 5 Conclusion, Discussion, and Recommendation

This final chapter is organized into three major parts. The first part presents the summary of findings, and the discussions of the findings. In the second part, pedagogical implications of the study, limitations of the study and recommendations for future research are explained. The last part ends with a conclusion of this chapter.

5.1 Research Summary

This English classroom motivation incentive teaching model aims to improve the English learning motivation of the learners by integrating the incentive teaching elements and building an incentive teaching environment in order to improve the learning effect. Through one semester's teaching experiment, the study examined the subjective feeling of the participants and objective effectiveness of the motivational model, including the learners' L2 learning motivation intensity and their academic performance before and after the experiment. In Chapter 4, both the quantitative and the qualitative findings were reported to answer the research questions on: (1) the effects of the motivational teaching model on the EFL learners' motivation toward learning English as a foreign language; (2) the effects of the motivational teaching model on the improvement of the EFL learners' language proficiency; (3) the effects of the motivational teaching model on the high/medium/low achievers in a heterogeneous class. The results were summarized as follows:

(1) The experimental group gained significantly in terms of motivational change toward learning English before and after the study. The learners under the motivational teaching model were more highly motivated in learning English as a foreign language than those in the control group. They tended to have more positive attitude toward this course, more confidence in learning and using English in and outside class, more enhanced ideal second language self and less anxiety in learning English.

(2) The experimental group made a significant improvement on their overall English proficiency in comparison with their counterparts in the control group. The language skills of speaking, translation and composition of the learners in the experimental group were superior to those in the control group. With regard to the listening and reading, the experimental group scored higher than their counterparts, but no significant difference was found between these two groups of learners.

(3) In addition to the whole-group comparisons, the effects of the motivational teaching model for learners with different initial levels of English achievement were also investigated. The results showed that the high achievers in the experimental group made a significant improvement on their overall English proficiency in comparison with their counterparts in the control group, and outperformed those in the control group in speaking and writing. The medium achievers improved significantly on their speaking, translation and writing compared with their counterparts in the control group, and performed as well as those in the control group in the overall proficiency. The low achievers progressed significantly in speaking, translation and writing in comparison with their counterparts in the control group and performed better in speaking and composition than those in the control group.

5.2 Discussion of the Overall Findings

The findings yielded in this study will also be discussed according to the research questions.

5.2.1 Effects of the Dynamic Motivational Teaching Model on Motivation

As presented previously, the learners in the treatment group demonstrated a much higher motivation at the end of the experiment compared to their counterparts in the control group. The motivational teaching model produced an obvious effect on the improvement of the L2 learners' attitude toward the English course, language learning confidence, situational anxiety, and L2 related ideal self. After much reflection and combined with the content in students' self-reports, the reasons for the enhanced motivation can be summarized as follows.

Firstly, this dynamic motivational teaching model integrated learning content with learning tasks, eliminating the traditional practice of learning for its own sake. Under the motivational model, the central role of output task was highlighted, as each unit began with the speaking and writing activity for students to complete, with the following teaching activities all revolving around this task. The advantages of doing this were that, on the one hand, students were equipped with a purpose of learning and a sense of direction which can lead to curiosity and passion, validated by research that the amount of time and effort one decides to invest in a particular task largely depended on the value the person attached to that task (Williams & Burden, 1997; Yuan, 2008). On the other hand, asking students to conduct the unit productive activities which were further divided into several sub-productive tasks can provide students with ample opportunity to use language, and motivate them to learn. As mentioned by students in their self-reports that they enjoyed learning something that could be put into practice. Language learning, to some extent, is to communicate. On the contrary, the artificial separation of learning the language from using the language which was common to see in the Chinese language learning classroom prevented student from appreciating the value of the effort, just as Dörnyei (2001) notes, "Indeed, one of the most demotivating factors for learners is when they have to learn something that they cannot see the point because it has no seeming relevance whatsoever to their lives."

In addition, under the dynamic motivational teaching model, the tasks were both challenging and able-do. For one thing, the tasks which were closely related with students' future study and lives posed students a challenge, and tasks that were intrinsically interesting and cognitively demanding would enhance students' motivation and lead to more and better opportunities for second language acquisition (Byrnes, 2000). After trying the productive activities, most students became aware of their insufficient abilities to complete the task. This could trigger a series of notice, prompting students to find clues from the teacher's future input to address language deficiencies (Swain, 1985), therefore, learners' initiative and motivation to acquire knowledge were enhanced. The increased score of Question 5 in the motivational questionnaire that "I am attentive to what the teacher says in English class." as shown in Table 4.4 can fully illustrate this point.

For another thing, under the motivational teaching model, all the learning materials and activities were closely pertinent to and served the productive tasks, helping the learners from less able to more able and finally better complete the assignments. As reported by Student 25, "The teacher asked our group to discuss the reading and listening materials and summarize what can be used in our productive task, while providing us with some useful words and expressions, which enables us to use what we have learned in hearing and reading directly for production", this can effectively reduce the difficulty of output and lessen students' anxiety in completing the output and protect the students' learning motivation. Due to the teacher's scaffolding represented by "big task, small steps" and the rich and varied authentic learning resources, students were entitled with a confidence that the task was able-do and the learning resources available were sufficient to succeed. The satisfaction and a feeling of well-being learners gained from their sense of progress could, according to the latest motivational theory (Dörnyei et al., 2014, 2015, 2016; Muir & Dörnyei, 2013), help students form a highly intense burst of motivation—the directed motivational current. Therefore, the dynamic motivational teaching model has the potential to increase the L2 learners' motivation.

Second, the learning material in the dynamic motivational model course was interesting and helpful. Different from the traditional English teaching which relied mainly on a single textbook, students under the motivational teaching model were exposed to a great variety of authentic materials with diverse ways to present them, including pictures, sound, animation, videos and other multimedia means. They enhanced learners' interest by providing an enriched learning environment (Yuan, 2008).

Although the worthy and challenging task aroused the learners' interest and motivation, it was the useful assistance from the teacher in terms of pertinent learning resources that can boost learners' confidence and let them know that the task can be fulfilled as long as they worked hard. This can be explained by the behaviour control theory (Ajzen, 1991; Duan, 2020), claiming that when the individual thinks he has more resources and opportunities and can expect success with fewer obstacles, he tends to consider the goals achievable and the process controllable. The greater this sense of control, the greater the motivation (Duan, 2020). After being assigned a task on speaking or writing, the students were provided with rich and diverse authentic materials including printed text, listening material, video clip, etc., from which they can acquire the necessary language, context and structure relevant to their productive tasks. Researchers also asserted that the more interesting and relevant the input material was, the happier were the students to accept and learn (Zhong, 2010).

Besides, the employment of the modern internet technology in this semester's English teaching also added convenience and zest in students' English learning, keeping the dullness at bay. Through Superstar Learning APP, students could download the audio and visual or reading materials uploaded by the researcher, as Student 14 said, "It gives us opportunities to make full use of our fragmented time to learn", "You learn, or don't, the materials are there, many of them are very fresh and interesting, so what is the reason not to learn?" This revealed that the teacher's use of E-learning to conduct the blended teaching could help students to shift from "passive learning" to "active learning". Apart from obtaining learning materials, the learners could also air their opinions for the questions online after class, and actively participate in the classroom teaching activities assisted by the multiple functions of the APP. Meanwhile, this APP could also facilitate the teacher to conduct the formative assessment on students by recording, evaluating and supervising students' learning process including in-class activities and extracurricular activities. The functions of "racing", "cloud map brainstorming", etc., not only improve teaching efficiency but also increase students' interest and prompt students to focus their attention longer in class (Wang, 2021). By using Writing Correction Online APP as a complement to peer correction and teacher correction, students can practice writing from multiple channels, which greatly improved students' interest in writing and enhanced their writing capability.

Thirdly, this motivational teaching model created a pleasant and relaxing learning context within which students enjoyed learning. This can be attributed to students' collaborative learning and the teacher's consistent use of motivational strategies. Dörnyei and Kubanyiova (2014) argue that group dynamics are so powerful that students would behave differently within the group from the way they do outside. The findings that cooperative learning could enhance learners' motivation in language learning were also supported by previous researches (Li & Gong, 2019). Under the dynamic motivational teaching model, students' frequent group interaction based on interdependence and accountability led to a mutual-support and mutual-caring learning atmosphere which can provide good conditions for students' social mental health and social skills (Li, 2007). Think-Pair-Share and the Adapted Jigsaw Reading were interesting and rewarding. Just as mentioned in students' self-reports, the collaborative learning created a more friendly and supportive learning context which entitled students to more opportunities and freedom to explore and practice their English. Through the Adapted Jigsaw Reading, students learned by teaching, which enhanced their autonomy and familiarity with the target language, just as a Chinese philosopher said, "Tell me, I forgot; show me, I understand; involve me, and I remember."

Deci and Ryan (1985) divide motivation into intrinsic/extrinsic motivation, while the intrinsic motivation was related to internal rewards like joy and self-satisfaction at performing a task, the extrinsic motivation was related to obtaining external rewards like marks and prizes. In the researcher's university, students' final score consists of the regular performance score and the final examination score. Through carrying out STAD, students were entitled to earn points as their regular performance score for their group by answering questions, making presentation in the classroom or expressing viewpoints via the online platform as suggested in Dörnyei's (2001) motivational teaching practice, "make sure that grades also reflect effort". This can greatly enliven the classroom atmosphere and increase students' initiative as shown in the increased score of Item 6 in Factor 2 of the motivational questionnaire "I often volunteer to answer questions in English lessons." after the treatment. Therefore, it was safe to say that cooperative learning in this teaching model can address students' intrinsic and extrinsic motivation.

As a most face-threatening thing when speaking a foreign language, anxiety could inhibit the learners' ability to process the language input (Krashen, 1985) as well as the output. Because of the increased amount of English talk and task participation in a natural, interactive environment created by cooperative learning, and knowing that solutions came from the group rather than from the individual, the students of the experimental group found more support, confidence and felt less embarrassed when they had to answer the questions or express his or her ideas in English in front of the class.

Apart from the emotional and academic support deriving from collaborative learning that help to create a pleasant and motivating learning environment, the teacher's consciously and consistent use of motivation strategies can also do its own part. Among these strategies, while some of which were displayed in the production tasks, learning material and collaborative learning as discussed above (such as facilitating learners linguistic confidence and motivation by providing them with more opportunities to use language, giving them more autonomy and responsibilities via collaborative group tasks and by exposing them to authentic learning materials via authentic videos and other engaging means, integrating Superstar Learning APP in and after class), there were still other motivation strategies along with positive, friendly and encouraging teacher behaviors that can also help to achieve this goal, and finally led to the enhanced students' L2 motivation. As the results shown in the students' self-reports, they observed the researcher's caring, supportive and motivated behaviours and they became more motivated. This was in line with many L2 motivation studies which argued that the teacher's motivation and enthusiasm had a substantial impact on students' L2 motivation (Dörnyei, 2001; Guilloteaux & Dörnyei, 2008, Erdil Z., 2016) as the teacher's efforts, preparedness and care were "contagious" and can infect students' motivation positively (Dörnyei & Kubanyiova, 2014; Dörnyei & Ushioda, 2011; Kubanyiova, 2006). Some students mentioned that they enjoyed learning English because the atmosphere in English class was enjoyable and they could learn a lot in the class.

Last but not the least, the inter- and intra-group comparison data of the motivational questionnaire demonstrated that the experimental group improved significantly both in the subscale Ideal Self and overall motivation, which proved that the ideal self could be seen as a strong indicator of students' motivation toward learning a foreign language. This finding ran counter to Wang and Dai's (2015) research which concludes that the learners' overall L2 learning motivation could not be increased accordingly with the enhanced ideal self. The reason may lie in not only facilitating students' creation of an attractive vision of an ideal language self but also helping them develop effective motivational self-guides (Dörnyei & Ushioda, 2011) to bridge the gap between the current self and future self. In this study, a series of idea language self intervention programs were designed first in the experimental group, then followed by action plan development and reflection. That is to say, students did not only need to construct a vivid and detailed mental image of their possible future ideal L2 self with a high proficiency in English, which was the prerequisite to launch their L2 learning motivation, but also needed to formulate their long-term and short-term goals in learning English, making attainable and measurable plans accordingly to reach the goal they had set. Such an immediate goal and action plan could help learners form the directed motivational current, once launched, the learners can enter an autonomous self-guide and can form a routine motivational behavior without a volitional control (Dörnyei, Muir & Ibrahim, 2014). They then also needed to reflect and assess regularly how well they had carried out their plan, from which they can perceive their own progress, obtain positive feedback, and continue to put into their efforts to continue the flow of motivation (Dörnyei, Ibrahim & Muir, 2015).

The results of the motivational questionnaire and students' reports indicated that the researcher's motivational teaching model had a positive influence on the motivation to learn English in the Chinese college English context. Compared with the learners in the regular college English class, those under the dynamic motivational teaching model demonstrated a stronger motivation to learn English. With a strong motivation to learn, it can be expected that the experimental group can achieve a remarkable progress in their language learning.

5.2.2 Effects of the Dynamic Motivational Teaching Model on Language Learning

As discussed previously, with an intense motivation to learn, the positive outcome in language learning would be a nature result to follow. The learners under the motivational teaching model in this study were found to be more highly motivated than those who studied in the regular college English class, and there was a significant difference in motivation to learn English between the two groups of learners. Correspondingly, after one semester's experimental teaching, learners under the motivational teaching model made a significant progress on their overall English proficiency involving speaking, listening, reading, translation and writing in the post-test compared to only one item (reading) found having a significant progress in the control group. The significant gains of the experimental group on the overall language proficiency supported the view that motivation was one of the key factors that determined L2 achievement and attainment (Cheng & Dörnyei, 2007), and such results were consistent with a growing body of literature claiming that learning motivation was positively interrelated with foreign language achievement. The higher the motivation, the more proficient they would become in the target language. (Luo, Jian & Wang, 2004; Meng, 2010). Indeed, the role that motivation plays in promoting learners to learn a language is huge. Only when learners have a strong learning motivation, can they actively think about "what" and "how to learn", formulate clear learning goals, overcome difficulties and take the initiative to seek knowledge. In students' self-reports, some of them revealed that since they received the unit productive task issued online by the researcher before the class, they began to think about how they should fulfil it. They would not only learn the visual and audio materials provided by the researcher but also browse the Internet to search for the relevant materials by themselves. In the classroom, the learners were found to listen attentively to the teacher and volunteer to answer as much as possible. With more time and efforts devoted to their learning of English, it is no wonder that the learners in the motivational teaching model can achieve better English proficiency.

The learners in the experimental group demonstrated a stronger ability on the language skills of speaking, writing and translation, indicating that the motivational teaching model improved the students' productive skills. The reasons to account for such phenomenon can be summarized as follows.

First, the experimental group was endowed with more opportunities to use the target language. This was partly due to the POA, and such findings were in compliance with Zhang's (2017) study that the POA can bring positive effects on learners' productive skills. There is no difficulty in explaining this. Under the POA, students were provided with more opportunities to use the target language by carrying out various communicative tasks in terms of both written and oral English. During one semester's treatment, there were altogether 5 units' productive activities, involving both oral and written tasks, and the former included one group presentation, one interview and one role play, and the latter one English letter and one composition essay. Each large productive task was further divided into several subtasks which also involved many oral and written practices. In contrast, the learners in the traditional class had fewer opportunities to use the target language to conduct the communicative task. What they focused was on the analysis of sentence structures and the usage of the new words in the text. Most of the learning tasks centred at the pattern drills instead of the real communication.

Apart from the various unit communicative tasks, in this study, the L2 Ideal Self program which required students to make a video using English to make suggestions to junior students, and composed their ideal self as well as their short-term plan and action plan (though not every student wrote in English, most of them chose to do so even though they were not required) also encouraged students to translate their ideas into English words. To provide students with more opportunities to practice their oral English, the students were encouraged to participate in the English corner on every Friday evening where two English speaking foreign teachers were also invited. This embodied the motivation Strategy 17 "Encourage students to use English outside the classroom" and Strategy 18 "Invite English-speaking foreigners to class" from the motivation inventory. Practice makes perfect, therefore students displayed a better oral communicative competence, as demonstrated in the results of this study.

In a cooperative learning context, the amount of students' target language practice was further maximized by interactive activity that involved pair work and group work, which engaged all the students in speaking. The language input, output, correction and meaningful communication happened during the group collaborative process can help learners deepen the processing of language knowledge, so as to improve their language ability and promote their cognitive development (Zhang, Zhou, 2021). Almost in each session of class, students were asked to do think-pair-share. The frequent interactive practice through pair or group work like the Adapted Jigsaw Reading, Round Robin Story Make-up and other oral productive activities might be an important factor contributing to the students' acquisition of oral communicative competence. This was also validated in students' self-reports where many students mentioned that under the POA and cooperative learning, the biggest improvement they found themselves made was oral English. Furthermore, cooperative learning also contributed to students' improvement of writing ability. Ideas and content for writing arouse from conducting teacher-students, and student-student interaction, which also prompted learners to reflect on language, discuss the language they were using, and collaborate in the solution of the linguistic problems they encountered (Dat T. V., 2014), In the assessment phase according to the POA, the self-correction and the peer-editing of students' written work, that is to say, writing and rewriting the same thing provided students with more opportunities to think, learn and polish, which led to the deepening cognition of the composition. This was also reflected in students' self-reports, for example, Student 12 mentioned that after three times revisions, she now had a better understanding of the framework and structure of a compositive article, and Student 31 reflected that he found his English writing expressive ability had been improved to a large degree.

The second reason for the experimental group's significant gains in the productive language may be due to their rich and sufficient exposure to authentic enabling materials in the forms of text, pictures, video and audio against the single form of text in the course book and lots of language exercises as the input for the control group. All these authentic materials (printed, visual and audial) not only enabled learners to interact with the language of native speakers, including its grammatical features, discourse structures, sociolinguistic features, and cultural referents (Biber, Conrad & Reppen, 1994; Kang, 2016), but also enhanced their awareness of appropriate and effective use of the target language. Many students reported that just because they read and listened much more than before, they could speak more fluently and write an English essay much longer and more easily than before. They could also put a lot of more new and idiomatic words in their oral communication as well as well-structured and beautifully complex sentences into their writings.

The third possible reason why the experimental group could make such a significant progress in productive competence was the affective factor, such as increased awareness, more confidence and less anxiety. This was true especially in terms of students' oral competence. Because the POA underscores the use of a language to do things (Wen, 2015), instead of just a course to pass the examination, most students have changed their perception about English and paid more attention to the productive skills—listening, writing and translation, which were their weak points compared to grammar and reading. When they increased their awareness and saw the point of using English to communicate, they were more willing to put into more time and energy into practicing this kind of skill, just as reflected in the large number of students taking initiative to participate in the English corner to practice their oral English.

In a supportive and less threatening learning context as provided by this motivational teaching model, students had more confidence and less anxiety in actively participating in the classroom oral activities and conduct peer interaction. They were more willing to volunteer to answer questions and express their ideas in and outside of the classroom, which made them access to ample opportunities to use their language skills and led to more improvement and achievement. Research finding shows that learners who perceive themselves as successful and capable learners can learn more and do better in school (Alexander, Kulikowich & Jetton, 1994; Yuan, 2008). Likewise, Clément also reports that self-confidence improves achievement (Clément, 1980; Wang, 2011). In this study, the POA, cooperative learning and teacher's using motivational strategy all helped to do their own parts.

After assigning the unit task, students were not only provided with the enabling materials but also the researcher's systematic guide, such as how to structure, how to cut into the main idea, how to make transition, or how to use the English language to express their ideas, etc., to lead them from being less to more able (Wen, 2016) and finally ensured that every student could complete the task with their efforts. And this can greatly help students to ease anxiety facing both the cognitive and language challenging task. The contribution of cooperative learning and motivation strategies in boosting students' confidence could find support from students' self-reports: "I used to be very shy and did not dare to speak in public, but with my group members' help and encouragement, I have become more and more outgoing and I never feel ashamed when I speak wrongly." " I don't feel embarrassed any longer when I make mistakes in speaking English because we are convinced by our teacher that we can always make progress by making mistakes."

From the three reasons above, it can be understood that students in the experimental group developed stronger speaking, writing and translation abilities than those in the control group. The motivational teaching model promoted the development of the productive skills of the experimental group.

The intra-group comparison demonstrated that the experimental group made a significant improvement in listening, while no such gains could be seen in the control group. This was not difficult to explain. Successful language development occurs when students are presented with materials in a meaningful context with a clear production purpose in mind (Yuan, 2008). In the present teaching experiment, the learners under the motivational teaching model were exposed to a large number of listening materials from which they could obtain the relevant ideas or useful language expressions. Besides, the students of the experimental group were required to take notes while they were listening to the talk show or other video clips in class. After listening, they were asked to do the information-gap activity or make comments on what they had heard. In contrast, without the production task as an orientation, there would be no impetus for the teacher to search for diverse input materials as a complement to enlarge students' language knowledge, and the listening practice was always limited to the CD-ROM of the textbook followed by the questions or multiple-choices based on what had been heard.

With regard to reading comprehension skills, both groups made a significant improvement in the post test, but with different reasons. For the experimental group, as with the listening materials, the learners were also exposed to a great number of reading materials, in order to identify what they needed for their language production, for example, the relevant ideas, language expression or discourse and structure to support their productive task, and students had to read extensively, which in turn brought the learners' sufficient comprehensible input. In addition, since the purpose of the input material was to help students to learn and produce, students had to read intensively and carefully in order to obtain crucial ideas from the text relevant to the productive activity, they had to learn how to identify and synthesize information which was an essential part of reading comprehension. To make good use of the language expression and discourse structure from the input materials, students had to read them repeatedly to realize a qualitative leap from language comprehension to production. Both the extensive and intensive reading could lead to students' significant gains in their reading comprehension skills.

For the control group, however, the significant progress may owe to their large amount of reading comprehension training with CET-4 as a driving force. For most freshmen, passing CET-4 has become their single aim of learning English since they entered the university, because for a long time, passing CET-4 has long been a necessary condition for college graduation and a prerequisite for large companies to recruit an employee in the present days. As an item with the one of the biggest score percentages in CET-4 test (writing

15%, listening 35%, reading 35%, translation 15%), it is fully understandable that students would place a high value and put a lot of effort and time in memorizing the new words and doing reading exercises as they always did in the exam-oriented traditional classroom, thus leading to their significant improvement in this language skill. The same explanation can also apply to the findings of listening comprehension (though there was a significant difference in within-group comparison in favour of the experimental group, the between-group comparison showed that no significant difference was identified between the two groups in the post-test) with the same score value in CET-4 test. Because the two groups of learners committed themselves to the listening and reading skill with similar efforts, that is why no significant difference could be found in terms of listening and reading between the two group in the post-test. Another possible reason for the finding was that under POA and cooperative learning, a great deal of attention was paid to the learners' productive skills and peer interaction, leaving little focus on specific receptive skills training, and even less on exam-orientation training. Furthermore, because the experimental teaching lasted for only one semester, the treatment effects may not be significantly obvious immediately in every language skill. According to the finding that "the higher the motivation, the more proficient they would become in the target language" (Meng, 2010; Ge & Jin, 2016). In other words, more gains of L2 learning motivation may finally lead to more gains of L2 proficiency progress, a sharper competitive edge in the listening and reading for the experimental group may emerge in the longer term.

In sum, the experimental group had a sharp edge in the productive skill, and in the meantime, still maintained a similar achievement in receptive skills as the control group. With such results, the motivational teaching model deserves more attention to increase students' overall language proficiency.

5.2.3 Effects of the Motivational Teaching Model on High/Medium/Low Achievers

As indicated in Chapter 4, the motivational teaching model had an impact on proficiency gains of learners with different levels of English proficiency, and the learners with a high level of proficiency made the most remarkable achievement compared with learners of the other two levels. Such findings were compatible with Zhang's (2017) research, who after a semester's empirical study of POA, also found that students of a high level of proficiency of the experimental group improved more significantly than students' of the other two levels when compared with the control group.

5.2.3.1 Effects of the Dynamic Motivational Teaching Model on High Achievers

The post-test in this study showed that the high achievers in the experimental group progressed significantly in each of the five language skills while no significant improvement can be found in the control group, and the high-achievers in the experimental group excelled those in the control group in their speaking and writing skills.

The high achievers in the experimental group revealed in their self-report that under the motivational teaching model, they had gradually changed their perception of learning English from pursuing high marks toward using it as a tool of communication. They were interested in the diverse communicative output tasks assigned at the start of each unit, which also posed a big challenge and enhanced this group students' motivation to learn and explore. Luckily, with all the required resources corresponding to the tasks uploaded on the online learning platform by the researcher, plus a solid English foundation they laid prior to college, the high achievers in the experimental group were in a unique position to choose what to learn and control their learning pace to serve for their production activity. Because the high achievers enjoyed more autonomy in learning, their initiative and independence were given full play, so that these students can maximize the learning effect in a free and relaxed atmosphere. Such tasks and challenges as well as the autonomy to learn what they needed, unfortunately, were rarely present in traditional classrooms. The high achievers in the control group, without ample opportunities to practice and use the target language, tended to be limited in their language development, thus leading to the so called "ceiling effect" (Zhang, 2017).

As reflected by students and observed by the researcher, during the cooperative learning, or group work, the high achievers in the experimental group were more active in the group work and talked longer in group discussion. They assumed more responsibilities to explain their ideas to their teammates and to lead the discussions. In this way, they were given plenty of opportunities not only to teach their classmates in the Adapted Jigsaw Reading as discussed previously, but also to teach their teammates in the discussion to enhance their understanding and learning. This benefited them a lot, as according to the Learning Pyramid, the retention rate could be as high as 50% in group discussion, and 90% in immediate use and teaching others. In contrast, the rate of lecturing which was the classic traditional way of learning could be as low as only 5%.

The high achievers in the experimental group were able to progress at their own pace, as the mastery of complex skills and abilities depended not only on learners' attention, retention, and motivation, but also on their awareness of self-efficacy and the self-regulatory system (Ryan & Deci, 2000). During the experimental teaching, the high achievers were found better at relating their English studies to their future possible selves, which provided both cohesion to their efforts and allowed the high achievers in the experimental group to focus their energies towards a clear finish line (Dörnyei Z., C. Muir & Z. Ibrahim, 2014). Therefore, they knew how to transform their goals into actions and self-monitor their process of learning via their study plan. Besides, they were able to take initiative and carry out their plans to the full, which led to their better self-directed behaviours. In this study, they were observed to volunteer to answer questions more frequently than groups of the other two levels of proficiency in class, and the online learning platform could also find them sharing their ideas in the target language more actively after class. In order to fulfil the output task with a high quality, apart from the textbook and materials provided by the researcher, they were also found to read English magazines and surf the Internet to explore more information, listen to English broadcasts or watch video to generate more ideas, translate some related materials in Chinese into English, and to practice repeatedly their oral tasks before presenting them in front of the whole class. After the teacher-and-student-collaborative assessment, they were also the group learners who were able to make an immediate revision after receiving teacher and peer' feedbacks on their production work. The high achievers in the experimental group devoted more time and effort to learning English which enabled them to make an overall improvement in various English language skills.

5.2.3.2 Effects of the Dynamic Motivational Teaching Model on Medium Achievers

The findings showed that the medium achievers in the experimental group made significant gains in speaking, translation and composition, while no significant progress was made by students of this level in the control group. Such gains can be explained by Vygotsky's (1978) zone of proximal development and Krashen's (1985) i+1 input hypothesis, because most of the medium achievers in the experimental group revealed in their self-reports that the rich enabling materials in various forms fulfilled their needs, which enabled them to make a bigger progress in speaking and writing. In Vygotsky's view (Lantolf & Thome, 2006; Lantolf J. P., 2011), all good learning should be just within the learners' zone of proximal, that is, the materials students learned should be just in advance of development and within their grasp in order to bridge the gap between the students' actual development level and their potential level. Krashen's i+1 also expressed the similar idea by saying that language acquisition took place when learners received language input that was comprehensible and just one step beyond their current stage of linguistic competence (Krashen, 1985). Sufficiently exposed to the enabling reading and listening materials carefully selected by the researcher that were pertinent to the output task, students were able to fully expand their knowledge and extend their skills to a higher level, and finally were able to complete the output speaking or writing activity assigned to them. In addition to the scaffolding from the instructor, group members also constitute a source of helping students across their zone of proximal as well as the i+1 input when students frequently conduct pair or group cooperative learning, where students are also able to learn from each other and co-construct knowledge together (Zhang, Zhou, 2021), for example, the peer-editing enables students to better realize their mistakes occurring in their production work and pushes them to revise and remember better.

Another reason why the medium group could make such significant gains in speaking, translation and writing, the productive skills so to speak, is that they experienced the facilitative anxiety (Brown, 2001; Yuan, 2008). Many students in this group mentioned that at the beginning, the new teaching model were so strange to them, plus there were so many big and small, challenging productive tasks to complete, and they found a little bit difficulty in totally understanding what the teacher said in English. All of these made them feel some anxiety. However, having a little nervous tension in the course of learning was a good thing just as argued by Brown (Yuan, 2008). Brown claimed that the facilitative anxiety, which the medium achievers experienced at the start of the teaching treatment, was one of the keys to success because it stimulated them to strengthen their effort to learn more. The following in and outside of classroom learning behaviours and the improvement percent in the post proficiency test and of the medium group did confirm this argument. The medium group were found to be able to conscientiously complete the speaking and writing production task, in addition, they were also observed to actively take part in the English corner to practice their oral English, and made fully prepared when it was their turn to make a presentation at the start of every class. The initial facilitative anxiety gave the medium achievers in the experimental group under the motivational teaching model enough tension, which in turn, drived them to work harder and achieve better. When they got the recognition and appreciation from teachers and peers, they felt their own progress and achieved a sense of gain which was an indispensable positive emotional state to maintain the flow of directional motivation (Duan, 2020; Dörnyei, Ibrahim & Muir, 2015)

However, compared to the improvement in every language skill of the high achievers in the experimental group, the medium did not progress significantly in listening and reading, nor did they excel this level of students in the control group significantly in any skill. Because the high school English learning focused on reading practice and emphasized text recitation. After entering the university, some students of a medium level of proficiency did not fully adapt to the selective learning advocated by POA, and the lack of attention to the textbooks and the accumulation of vocabulary led to their no big progress found in reading ability. For example, Student 20 wrote in his self-report, "There are too many English learning resources around me, and I begin to unconsciously neglected textbooks. I think it is very necessary to learn textbooks, and I will spend some effort in textbooks in the future." Still some students in the experimental group confided that the new teaching model involved so many speaking and writing productive work which called for students' autonomy and group cooperation to complete outside the classroom. Student 4 confessed his regret at the end of a semester, "I find the motivational teaching model is fantastic. I can acquire a lot if I am fully engaged, however, as it is the first time I left home, free from the supervision of parents and my class advisor, I have much money and time at my disposal. I am kind of self-indulge myself, and do not make a good control of my learning." Student 15 wrote that she was more used to the traditional classroom where the teacher lectured the textbook in front of class and students took notes at their seats. She expected the teacher spent more time on grammar and sentences explanation rather than asking students to teach and on other pair and group work.

5.2.3.3 Effects of the Dynamic Motivational Teaching Model on Low Achievers

The low achievers in the experimental group also scored significantly in their post-test higher than the pre-test in speaking, translation and writing, while no such gains can be found by students of this level in the control group.

Some low achievers in the experimental group reflected they did not like learning English because since they began to learn English in the secondary school, the focus of classroom was to memorize vocabulary and practice grammatical structure, which was so boring and so challenging to their memory. Under the motivational teaching model, however, the emphasis of the practical use of language could arouse their interest and passion toward learning English, because as adults, they preferred to the target-driven learning when they were clearly informed the potential value of the learning task (Wen, 2017). Furthermore, since the learners were able to put what they just learned into an immediate use, they can reap a lot academically, because as mentioned previously about the Learning Pyramid, the retention rate of immediate use, just as learning by teaching, can be as high as 90%. It was found from the low achievers' post-tests that the vocabulary and fluency in their oral test were remarkably improved, and the quality of students' compositions in structure, coherence, sentence type and collocation were also greatly enhanced. In contrast, instead of improving in the post-test writing, the score of the low achievers in the control group even dropped significantly in the post-written test.

In addition, the significant gains in speaking, overall written test, and writing in particular, of the low achievers in the experimental group could partially be explained by Vygotsky's theory of cognitive development, according to which, an essential feature of learning was that it awakened a variety of internal developmental processes that were able to operate only when the learner was in the action of interacting with people in his or her environment and in cooperation with his or her peers. Applying to the language learning in this study, the cooperative learning, taking the "Teacher and Student Collaborative Assessment" for example, enabled the low achievers in the experimental group to make and receive comments on each other's productive work from their pair, and to improve their work according to peer's suggestion, thus leading to their consistent progress. In such supportive and beneficial learning context, students of this group were able to take more challenging tasks, use more effective strategies, perform better in face of obstacles, and to feel much empowered, and were intrinsically motivated after successfully finishing their group work.

This group of learners also stated in the self-reports that they found the Ideal Language Self project very helpful. Student 56 revealed, "Although I knew English was very important, I did not really think about what English can help me in the future before. The idea of 'L2 ideal self' makes me clarify how English can relate me in my future life and career, and now I feel more motivated in English learning." Once learners changed their possible selves, this can lead to the positive changes in academic behaviour, in better academic performance and lower risk of depression (Lee & Oyserman, 2009).

Student 21 said that she had learnt to regulate her English learning according to her short-term and long-term goals, whenever she was lazy or distracted by other things, it was her future-oriented goals that urged her to focus her attention, exert more effort and to persist longer.

5.3 Pedagogical Implications

How to arouse the interest and stimulate the imagination of the students so as to motivate students to learn is still one of the biggest challenges facing language teachers every day. By embedding motivation strategies into three vital elements in the process of L2 teaching—teaching method, teaching organization and teaching means, this motivation-oriented teaching model creates a motivational environmental system, with its four parts interacting with one another to exert a positive influence on students' L2 motivation and language proficiency development. The POA enables students to see clearly the relevance of learning the target language. It first engages students in real-world and challenging activities and then exposes them to abundant input materials. It not only fully generates students' desire to learn actively, but also helps them to successfully complete these tasks and leads to their boosted confidence. Under the POA, learners have opportunities to make choices in the content and the learning activities from the abundant learning materials, thus they can take an active role in the learning process which develops their self-autonomy.

Cooperative learning facilitates peer interactions, thus by listening to one another, asking questions and explaining their reasoning, cooperative learning helps improve oral communication skills. Because this teaching technique increases students' participation and makes them more active in the classroom, their satisfaction with the learning experience is enhanced. What is more, cooperative learning nurtures a friendly and supportive environment within which ideas and solutions come from the group collective wisdom rather than the individual fighting alone, making students feel more secure and less anxious.

The use of a wide range of semiotic modes in materials and activities, such as printed text, music, pictures, videos, games and online learning APP, etc., in the teaching process not only makes English learning colourful and vivid, stimulating students interests in learning, but also improves their English language ability, facilitating them to directly feel the knowledge of British and American culture and custom. In this study, 34 motivational strategies selected from Dörnyei's motivational teaching practice and activities based on L2MSS ran through the whole teaching process; some were already displayed in the three vital elements of teaching, while there were still some other applied as complement.

Among these motivation strategies that might offer pedagogical implications for the L2 classroom is that teacher is the most important factor on learner motivation (Dörnyei, 2001; Dörnyei & Ushioda, 2011). Therefore, it is critical for the L2 teachers to get out of the comfort zone and dedicate themselves to teaching so that they can expect students do the same way in learning. While adopting the POA, in order to select the appropriate materials to match the task, the teacher may need to spend a lot of time and energy surfing the Internet and searching for the wide variety of materials to meet the requirements of students of different levels of language proficiency. In order to help students to complete the productive task, it also requires the teacher to frequently cooperate with students and collect their feedbacks from the beginning toward the end of the teaching process. Only in this way, can the teacher get the first hand of students' difficulty and the gap between their current ability and target requirements in the cognitive structure and the language level of the productive task, then the teacher can provide a timely support to guide students to move forward to the goal. They can also make an immediate diagnostic and a remedial teaching after students finishes each subtask designed by the teacher.

While carrying out the Adapted Jigsaw Reading in cooperative learning, the teacher's work is by no means less, if not more, because the teacher has to take multiple roles as organizer, commentator and facilitator. As different groups take charge of different learning parts, such as text structure, vocabulary or writing style, a carefully designed teaching plan with clearly stated procedures and activities should be prepared in advance by the teacher, and given to the group who are to assume the given responsibility to teach. While teaching in front of the class, the students are also required to make PPT to accompany their oral presentation, and design exercises for students to do in order to examine their teaching effects. Three groups are the maximum for a period of class with the time allowed for one group no more than 15 minutes. After the group presentation, the teacher would be expected to give immediate feedbacks, make comments, give scores and above all, to make corrections and supplements when necessary.

In multimodal teaching, taking into consideration the students' desire for more interesting lessons, the teacher should make full use of various media and teaching resources, especially the online learning resources. In addition to Superstar Learning APP adopted in this study, teachers can also encourage students to learn their vocabulary through human-computer interaction, and complete the corresponding listening and learning activities independently. Teachers can also use the correcting network and I-write system, to help with writing and translation teaching. Meanwhile, during the classroom teaching, the different modes (pictures, video, audio, etc.) are by no means simply amassed, but should coordinate and complement each other, making one modal structure as a dominant mode, and the other taking the second place when designing the teaching activities, so as not to distract students and to gain the maximum teaching effects.

5.4 Limitations and Recommendations

Despite some positive findings yielded in this study to claim the effectiveness of the motivational teaching model in terms of students' L2 motivation and academic achievements, and the researcher has made great efforts in the process of teaching design and implementation, there are still some pity and limitations which might be improved in the future study.

(1) 142 participants were involved in this particular study with 72 in the experimental group and 70 in the control group. However, due to the conditional limit of the oral test, it was a pity that there were only 42 students from each group, altogether 84 students participated and in the oral and written test. Besides, the samples of the participants were restricted to only two classes of the freshmen in Anhui Polytechnic University. Due to adopting production-oriented as its teaching method which required students have a moderate high level of English, thus the study results might not apply to other schools or other majors, such as art students with a relatively poor English foundation. In addition, in this study, only the learners in the course of Comprehensive English were selected as the samplers. In the future studies, more studies on student participants of different majors and levels of proficiency as well as from different English courses are recommended, thus generating more evidence on the effects of the motivational teaching model.

(2) This experimental teaching study only lasted less than 4 months, therefore, it was difficult to significantly improve all the language skills in such limited time. For some motivational strategies, such as the vision strengthening activities, there might be a "time-lag" phenomenon, that is, the treatment may not be obvious immediately. Instead, it will emerge in the longer term. To achieve better experimental results, extended future experimental research periods are recommended. Moreover, the data collected for the analysis of the students' speaking ability was based on a total score

of an IELTS oral test, no detailed competence analysis was conducted in this study such as pronunciation, vocabulary, grammar and fluency. With time and funding permitted, future study measuring students' oral performance from the four aspects is recommended to get a better understanding of the impact of the teaching model on the change of students' oral communicative competence.

(3) The purpose of this study is to enhance students' L2 learning motivation and their practical use ability of English. However, due to the college English teaching situation in China, the number of students in one class means that it not only increases the workload of teachers (such as reviewing students' composition, etc.), but also because of the great divergence of students' English level, it weakens the pertinence of teaching and limits the effect of the motivational teaching model. What is more, as a brand-new teaching theory, the POA posts a great challenge to the researcher, due to the lack of available teaching materials to match it, most of the time was spent on the teaching design and surfing the Internet to search for the suitable input, leaving limited time for giving more care to and developing personal relationships with students, which, in my view, is vital to be a motivating teacher.

5.5 Conclusion

China is in urgent need of a large number of professionals with a strong foreign language ability. In order to deepen the reform of college English teaching and improve the teaching quality, the Guideline of College English Teaching (2017) points out that college English teaching should be oriented by the practical use of English, and focus on cultivating students' English application ability which refers to the ability to communicate in English in the study, life and future work. By implementing the motivational teaching model for one semester, we are convinced that it is an ideal model which holds a great promise for accelerating students' attainment of both the acquisition and practical use of English knowledge, motivation to learn, and the development of the knowledge and abilities necessary for needs of the national English talents as well as the personal needs for future study, employment and life. All in all, there are three conclusions made in response to the research questions based on the research findings.

The motivational teaching model has an impact on learners' motivation. The L2 learners have a more positive attitude towards the college English course as their needs of both the acquisition and use of language are satisfied. The ample opportunities to use and improve the target language in the classroom with teacher's encouraging feedbacks bring learners' more positive emotional experience. Frequent interactions with group members in English and an emphasis on cooperation rather than competition empower learners to present their work in front of the class more confidently and they tend to feel less anxious when expressing themselves in English. Students under the motivational teaching model display a strong desire to learn English, and take a more active role in the learning process.

Due to the researcher's consistent and systematic use of motivation strategy, this motivational teaching model provides a caring and supportive environment in and outside of the classroom that makes English learning more pleasant, lively and encouraging, which leads to students' enhanced L2 learning motivation. In such a motivational context as the treatment class, the focus of language learning is on the use rather than on the language itself and what they have done is "learning by doing" rather than "learning by taking notes". Realizing that what they learned was of relevance to their future career and study, and was worth the effort to do, the students collaborated with the teacher and their peer team members very well, which in turn developed students' academic, personal and social growth. This enabled them to overcome all the difficulties in the process of completing the productive activities, and enhanced their confidence in future English learning and using as this motivational teaching model continued.

Motivation and achievements are closely correlated. The results indicated that once students' motivation in English learning was stimulated, their accomplishment in their language would be naturally followed. Students' productive skills including speaking, translation and writing developed significantly and learners felt more confident in using English to communicate due to their frequent use in the motivational teaching model classroom. Learners' receptive skills including listening comprehension and reading comprehension were also enhanced as they were exposed to a variety of task-pertinent materials and to a considerable amount of language input. They learned useful language that was embedded within relevant discourse contexts instead of isolated language fragments. This carefully selected language materials by the researcher were comprehensible and linked to their proximal previous learning, which was essential for successful language acquisition. Under the motivational teaching model, both the teacher and learners explored content in the rich and various forms, with the authentic and meaningful content and language, which promoted language learning. They were entitled to lots of opportunities to practice listening, speaking, reading, translation and writing when they completed various speaking and writing tasks. In the process of doing this, the learners learned both individually and socially from others. When they were engaged in the learning materials and activities, they had to discover the useful content and language items by themselves. During social interactions, scaffolding provided by the teacher and peer group members also led to efficient learning.

The motivational teaching model is a feasible teaching method that enables students with various levels of English proficiency to make a significant improvement in the productive language skills while does not hinder their progress in receptive language skills. This is a model that makes it possible for students with diverse abilities to discover language through real use and practice rather than telling them about language. Under the model, students go into the depth of the input to acquire more useful and deeper knowledge, actively interact with the teacher and peers and construct their own knowledge, have a higher sense of self-determination to make progress at their own pace, and at the same time, contribute to their peers' learning. In such a learning-oriented teaching model, students with a high level of proficiency are encouraged and motivated to explore and discover more other than the input provided by the teacher outside the classroom, and students of the medium and low levels can enjoy the listening and speaking activities in a friendly and non-threatening atmosphere, altogether moving on to the zone of proximal development.

References

AJZEN I, 1991. The theory of planned behavior[J]. Organizational behavior and human decision processes, 50: 179-211.

ALCIONE, OSTORGA N, ESTRADA V L, 2009. Impact of an action research instructional model: student teachers as reflective thinkers[J]. Action in teacher education, 30（4）: 18-27.

ALEXANDER P A, KULIKOWICH J M, JETTON T L, 1994. The role of subject-matter knowledge and interest in the processing of linear and nonlinear texts[J]. Review of educational research, 64: 201-252.

AU S Y, 1988. A critical appraisal of Gardner's social-psychological theory of second-language （L2） learning[J]. Language learning, 38（1）: 75-99.

BERNAUS M, GARDNER R C, 2008. Teacher motivation strategies, student perceptions, student motivation, and English achievement[J]. Modern language journal, 92（3）: 387-401.

BIBER D, CONRAD S, REPPEN R, 1994. Corpus-based approaches to issues in applied linguistics[J]. Applied linguistics, 15: 169-189.

BÖLÜKBA F B, KESKIN F, POLAT M, 2011. The effectiveness of cooperative learning on the reading comprehension skills in Turkish as a foreign language[J]. Turkish online journal of educational technology, 10（4）: 330-335.

BROWN H, 2015. Teaching by principles: an interactive approach to language pedagogy[M]. 4th ed. White Plains, NY: Pearson Education.

BRUFFEE K A, 1995. Sharing our toys: cooperative learning versus collaborative learning[J]. Change, 27（1）: 12-18.

BYRNES H, 2000. Languages across the curriculum: intradepartmental curriculum construction: issues and options[M]//KECHT M R, HAMMERSTEIN K. Languages across the curriculum: interdisciplinary structures and internationalized education. Columbus, OH: The Ohio State University Press.

CAI J G, 2010. Some thoughts on reorientation of college English teaching in China[J]. Foreign language teaching and research, 4: 306-308.

CAI J G, 2012. What is the future of Chinese college English teaching?[M]. Shanghai: Shanghai Jiao Tong University Press.

CAO M, BAI L S, 2018. Cooperative learning process model and application for mathematical solving[J]. Electrochemical education research（11）: 85-91.

CAO P S, 2012. Experimental study on the effectiveness of college English CBI subjects[J]. Foreign language telecommunications teaching（3）: 5.

CAO Q Z, 2017. An analysis of the role of teachers in output-oriented approach: a case study of the fourth unit of new generation college English[J]. Chinese foreign language education（1）: 15-22.

CAO S R, 2017. Teaching practice of English phonetics course based on the "production-oriented method"[J]. Journal of Bengbu college（2）: 138-142.

CAO Y M, 2018. A research on demotivation of freshmen of non-English major in English learning[D]. Guilin: Guangxi Normal University.

CHAMBERS G N, 1999. Motivating language learners[M]. Bristol: Multilingual Matters.

CHANG X L, 2017. Research on textbook compilation based on POA[J]. Modern foreign languages, 40（3）: 359-362.

CHEN J L, 2010. Integration of computer networks and foreign language courses: a study based on college English teaching reform[M]. Shanghai: Shanghai Foreign Language Education Press.

CLÉMENT R, 1980. Ethnicity, contact and communicative competence in a second language[M]//GILES H, ROBINSON W P, SMITH P M. Language: social psychological perspectives. Oxford: Pergamon Press Ltd.

CLÉMENT R, DÖRNYEI Z, NOELS K A, 1994. Motivation, self-confidence, and group cohesion in the foreign language classroom[J]. Language learning, 44 (3): 417-448.

CLINTON G, HOKANSON B, 2012. Creativity in the training and practice of instructional designers: the design/creativity loops model[J]. Educational technology research and development, 6 (1): 111-130.

CORNO L, 1994. Implicit teachings and self-regulated learning[J]. Educational environment (4): 4-22.

CRESWELL J, 2015. Educational research: planning, conducting, and evaluating quantitative and qualitative research[M]. London: Pearson Education, Inc.

CROOKES G, SCHMIDT R W, 1991. Motivation: reopening the research agenda[J]. Language learning, 41 (4): 469-512.

CSIZÉR K, DÖRNYEI Z, 2005. Language learners' motivational profiles and their motivated learning behavior[J]. Language learning, 55 (4): 613-659.

CSIZÉR K, KORMOS J, 2009. Learning experiences, selves and motivated learning behaviour: a comparative analysis of structural models for Hungarian secondary and university learners of English[M]// DÖRNYEI Z, USHIODA E. Motivation, language identity and the L2 self. Bristol: Multilingual Matters.

DAT T V, 2014. The effects of cooperative learning on the academic achievement and knowledge retention[J]. International journal of higher education, 3（2）：131-140.

DAVIS R L, 1997. Group work is not busy work：maximizing success of group strategies for implementing interaction in college English class work in the L2 classroom[J]. Foreign language annals （2）：265-277.

DECI E L, 2004. Intrinsic motivation and self-determination in human behavior[J]. Encyclopedia of applied psychology, 3（2）：437-448.

DECI E L, RYAN R M, 1985. Intrinsic motivation and self-determination in human behavior[M]. New York：Springer.

DÖRNYEI Z, 1994. Motivation and motivating in the foreign language classroom[J]. Modern language journal, 78（3）：273-284.

DÖRNYEI Z, 2001. Motivational strategies in the language classroom[M]. Cambridge：Cambridge University Press.

DÖRNYEI Z, 2005. The psychology of the language learner：individual differences in second language acquisition[M]. New York：Lawrence Erlbaum.

DÖRNYEI Z, 2009. Motivation, language identity and the L2 self [M]. Bristol：Multilingual Matters.

DÖRNYEI Z, CHAN L, 2013. Motivation and vision：an analysis of future L2 self images, sensory styles, and imagery capacity across two target languages[J]. Language learning, 63（3）：437-462.

DÖRNYEI Z, CSIZÉR K, 1998. Ten commandments for motivating language learners：results of an empirical study[J]. Language teaching research, 2（3）：203-229.

DÖRNYEI Z, IBRAHIM Z, MUIR C, 2015. "Directed motivational currents"：regulating complex dynamic systems through motivational surges[M]//DÖRNYEI Z, MACINTYRE P D, HENRY A. Motivational dynamics in language learning. Bristol：Multilingual Matters.

DÖRNYEI Z, KUBANYIOVA M, 2014. Motivating learners, motivating teachers[M]. Cambridge: Cambridge University Press.

DÖRNYEI Z, MALDEREZ A, 1997. Group dynamics and foreign language teaching[J]. System, 25 (1) : 65-81.

DÖRNYEI Z, MUIR C, IBRAHIM Z, 2014. Directed motivational currents: energising language learning by creating intense motivational pathways[M]//LASAGABASTER D, DOIZ A, SIERRA J M. Motivation and foreign language learning: from theory to practice. Amsterdam: John Benjamins.

DÖRNYEI Z, OTTO I, 1998. Motivation in action: a process model of L2 motivation[J]. Working papers in applied linguistics (Thames Valley University, London), 4 (43) : 43-69.

DÖRNYEI Z, USHIODA E, 2009. Motivation, language identity and the L2 self[M]. Bristol: Multilingual Matters.

DÖRNYEI Z, USHIODA E, 2011. Teaching and researching motivation[M]. 2nd ed. London: Pearson Education.

DOUGHTY C, PICA T, 1986. Information gap tasks: do they facilitate second language acquisition?[J]. TESOL quarterly, 20 (2) : 305-325.

DUAN Y L, 2020. A study of L2 motivational intervention in blended teaching settings[J]. Foreign language education in China, 3 (4) : 49-56.

DUAN Z Z, 2004. Curriculum reform and teaching mode transformation[J]. Educational research (6) : 67-71.

EISENKRAFT A, 2003. Expanding the 5E model[J]. Science teacher, 70 (1) : 150-169.

ERDIL Z, 2016. Promoting L2 motivation via motivational teaching practice: a mixed-methods study in the Turkish EFL context[D]. Tampa, Florida: University of South Florida.

GAGNE R M, 1977. The condition of learning[M]. 3rd ed. Saint Louis, MO: Rinehart and Winston.

GARDNER R C, 1985. Social psychology and second language learning:
the role of attitudes and motivation[M]. London: Edward Arnold.

GARDNER R C, LAMBERT W E, 1959. Motivational variables in second
language acquisition[J]. Canadian journal of psychology, 13: 266-272.

GASS S M, MACKEY A, 2006. Input, interaction and output[J]. Aila
review, 19 (1): 3-17.

GE N N, JIN L X, 2016. Empirical study on the relationship between two-
language motivation self-system and English learning effectiveness[J].
Foreign language journal (5): 122-126.

GILLIES R M, ASHMAN A F, 2000. The effects of cooperative learning
on students with learning difficulties in the lower elementary school[J].
Journal of special education, 34 (1): 19-27.

GOMLEKSIZ M N, 2007. Effectiveness of cooperative learning (jigsaw
II) method on teaching English as a foreign language to engineering
students (case of Fiat University, Turkey) [J]. European journal of
engineering education, 32 (5): 613-625.

GU Y G, 2007. Multimedia and multimodal learning analysis[J]. Foreign
language telecommunications teaching (2): 3-13.

GUILLOTEAUX M J, DÖRNYEI Z, 2008. Motivating language learners:
a classroom-oriented investigation of the effects of motivational strategies
on student motivation[J]. TESOL quarterly, 42: 55-77.

HAO Z J, XU J C, 2003. 20 years of teaching mode research: course,
problems and direction[J]. Educational theory and practice (23): 52-
56.

HECKHAUSEN H, KUHL J, 1985. From wishes to action: the dead ends
and short cuts on the long way to action[M]//FRESE M, SABINI J. Goal-
directed behaviour: the concept of action in psychology. New York:
Lawrence Erlbaum.

Higher Education Department, Ministry of Education, China, 2007.

College English course teaching requirements[M]. Beijing: Higher Education Press.

HOCK M F, SCHUMARKER J B, DESHLER D D, 2002. Draft of possible selves strategy instruction manual[J]. Personal communication, 16 (1): 7.

HODGE R, KRESS G, 1988. Social semiotics[M]. Cambridge: Polity Press.

HU J, 2005. Research on student independent inquiry learning and its teaching mode under the network environment[J]. Electrical education research (1): 76-80.

HU Y J, ZHANG D L, 2013. Experimental study on multimodal function in English listening teaching[J]. The foreign language community (5): 7.

HU Z L, 2007. Multimodality in social semiotics studies[J]. Language teaching and research (1): 52-55.

HUBERMAN A M, MILES M B, 1994. Qualitative data analysis: a sourcebook of new methods[M]. Thousand Oaks, CA: Sage Publications.

JENSEN M, JOHNSON D W, JOHNSON R T, 2002. Impact of positive interdependence during electronic quizzes ondiscourse and achievement[J]. The journal of educational research, 95 (3): 161-166.

JI M Y, 2004. Investigation on the use of motivational strategies for English teachers in teaching[J]. Foreign language community (6): 34-40.

JOHNSON D W, JOHNSON R T, 1999. Making cooperative learning work[J]. Theory into practice, 38 (2): 67-73.

JOYCE B, WEIL M, CALHOUN E, 2004. Models of teaching[J].7th ed. Boston, MA: Allyn and Bacon.

KAGAN S, 1994. Cooperative learning[M]. Clemente, CA: Kagan Publishing.

KANG L M, 2016. English teaching design of college athletes from multimodal semiotic[J]. Journal of Wuhan institute of physical education, 50（10）：90-95.

KAPLAN A, GARNER J K, BROCK B, 2019. Identity and motivation in a changing world: a complex dynamic systems perspective: theory, research, and implications for practice[J]. Motivation in education at a time of global change, 20: 101-127.

KILBANE C R, MILMAN N B, 2014. Teaching models: designing instruction for 21st century learners[M]. London: Pearson.

KORMOS J, CSIZÉR K, 2008. Age-related differences in the motivation of learning English as a foreign language: attitudes, selves, and motivated learning behavior[J]. Language learning, 58（2）：327-355.

KRASHEN S D, 1985. The input hypothesis: issues and implications[M]. London: Addison-Wesley Longman Ltd.

KRESS G, 2003. Literacy in the new media age[M]. New York: Routledge.

KRESS G, VAN LEEUWEEN T, 2001. Colourasa semiotic mode: notes for a grammar of colour[J]. Visual communication, 1（3）：343-368.

KUBANYIOVA M, 2006. Developing a motivational teaching practice in EFL teachers in Slovakia: challenges of promoting teacher change in EFL contexts[J]. TESL-EJ, 10（2）：1-17.

KYNDT E, RAES E, LISMONT B, et al., 2013. A meta-analysis of the effects of face-to-face cooperative learning. Do recent studies falsify or verify earlier findings? [J]. Educational research review, 10（1）：133-149.

LANTOLF J P, 2011. The sociocultural approach to second language acquisition: sociocultural theory, second language acquisition, and artificial L2 development[M]//ATKINSON D. Alternative approaches to second language acquisition. New York: Routledge.

LANTOLF J P, THORNE S, 2006. Sociocultural theory and the genesis of second language development[M]. Oxford: Oxford University Press.

LEE S J, OYSERMAN D, 2009. Possible selves theory[J]. Reference reviews, 23（8）: 23-30.

LEMKE J, 2002. Travels in hypermodality[J]. Visual communication, 1（3）: 299-325.

LI B M, GONG L L, 2019. Research on the influence of cooperative learning on students' learning achievements: based on meta-analysis of 54 experimental studies or quasi-experimental studies at home and abroad[J]. Research on education development, 39（24）: 39-47.

LI J L, 2007. Empirical research on the feasibility of cooperative learning in university English large class teaching[J]. Journal of Xi'an international studies university（3）: 91-94.

LI L, 2004. On the exploration and theoretical innovation of teaching model[J]. Journal of educational plexus, Guangdong radio and television university（4）: 7-10.

LI Z, 2017. Practical research of production-oriented approach in English flipped classroom in vocational colleges[J]. Chinese vocational and technical education（31）: 5.

LI Z Z, 2003. Social symbolic analysis of multimodal discourse[J]. Foreign language study（5）: 59.

LINCOLN Y S, GUBA E G, 1985. Naturalistic inquiry Sage[M]. Thousand Oaks, CA: Sage Publications.

LIU L M, 2010. A study of the feasibility of collaborative learning on English writing teaching in higher vocational college[J]. China vocational and technical education（2）: 72-75.

LIU M, HU J S, 2010. Multimodal design concept and requirements analysis of university foreign language audio-visual teaching materials[J]. Foreign language telecommunications teaching（2）: 52.

LONG M, 1996. The role of the linguistic environment in second language acquisition[M]//ITCHIE W R, BHATIA T K. Handbook of second language acquisition. Washington, DC: Academic Press.

LUO J W, JIAN X M, WANG Y F, 2004. Research on the relationship between learning motivation[J]. Foreign language learning strategies and academic achievement, teaching research（2）: 146-151.

MACINTYRE P D, 2002. Motivation, anxiety and emotion in second language acquisition[M]//ROBINSON P. Individual differences and instructed language learning. Amsterdam: John Benjamins.

MAGID M, 2014. An application of the L2 motivational self system to motivate elementary school English learners in Singapore[J]. Journal of education and training studies, 2（1）: 228-237.

MAGID M, CHAN L, 2012. Motivating English learners by helping them visualise their ideal L2 self: lessons from two motivational programmes[J]. Innovation in language learning and teaching, 6（2）: 113-125.

MARKUS H, NURIUS P, 1986. Possible selves[J]. American psychologist, 41（9）: 954-969.

MENG D M, 2010. Teaching design English classroom motivation incentive [D]. Shanghai: Shanghai Foreign Studies University.

MUIR C, DÖRNYEI Z, 2013. Directed motivational currents: using vision to create effective motivational pathways[J]. Studies in second language learning and teaching, 3: 357-375.

New London Group, 1996. A pedagogy of multiliteracies: designing social futures[J]. Harvard educational review, 66（1）: 60-92.

NOELS K A, 2001. Learning Spanish as a second language: learners' orientations and perceptions of their teachers' communication style[J]. Language learning, 51（1）: 107-144.

NOELS K A, CLEMENT R, PELLETIER L G, 1999. Perceptions of teachers' communicative style and students' intrinsic and extrinsic motivation[J]. Modern language journal, 83: 23-34.

O'HALLORAN K L, 2004. Multimodal discourse analysis: systemic-functional perspectives[M]. New York: Continuum.

PAPI M, 2010. The L2 motivational self system, L2 anxiety, and motivated behavior: a structural equation modeling approach[J]. System, 38 (3): 467-479.

QI P, SHI X C, 2016. The course design of English visual and speaking based on POA and the study on its effectiveness[J]. Academic month of education (8): 106-111.

QIU L, 2017. A study on the process design of language enabling links in POA[J]. Modern foreign languages (3): 386-396, 439.

RABAA K, ALMOMEN, 2016. Applying the ADDIE: analysis, design, development, implementation and evaluation: instructional design model to continuing professional development for primary care physicians in Saudi Arabia[J]. International journal of clinical medicine, 7 (8): 538-546.

RAFFINI J P, 2010. 150 ways to increase intrinsic motivation in the classroom[J]. Contemporary clinical trials, 31 (6): 624-633.

ROYCE T, BOWCHER W, 2007. New directions in the analysis of multimodal discourse[M]. New York: Lawrence Erlbaum Associates.

RYAN R M, DECI E L, 2000. Self-determination theory and the facilitation of intrinsic motivation, social development, and well-being[J]. American psychologist, 55: 68-78.

RYAN S, 2009. Self and identity in L2 motivation in Japan: the ideal L2 self and Japanese learners of English[M]//DÖRNYEI Z, USHIODA E. Motivation, language identity and the L2 self. Bristol: Multilingual Matters.

SAMPSON R, 2012. The language-learning self, self-enhancement activities, and self perceptual change[J]. Language teaching research, 16 (3): 317-335.

SENEMOĞLU N, 2002. Geli im, ö renme ve ö retim: kuramdan

uygulamaya （Development，learning and instruction） [M]. Ankara：
Gazi Kitapevi.

SHINICHI I，2002. Output，input enhancement，and the noticing
hypothesis：an experimental study on ESL relativization[J]. Studies in
second language acquisition，24：541-577.

SLAVIN R E，1980. Student team learning[J]. Academic achievement，25：
10-12.

SLAVIN R E，1995. Cooperative learning：theory，research，and
practice[M]. 2nd ed. Boston，MA：Allyn and Bacon.

SMITH K A，SHEPPARD S D，JOHNSON D W，et al.，2005. Pedagogies
of engagement：classroom-based practices[J]. Journal of engineering
education，94（1）：87-101.

STRAUSS A L，1987. Qualitative analysis for social scientists[M].
Cambridge：Cambridge University Press.

SU Y C，2019. Analysis on the reliability and validity of university
English[J]. Overseas English language （16）：130.

SUN S G，2017. An empirical classroom reflective research on "collaborative
assessment of teachers and students" [J]. Modern foreign language （3）：
397-406，439.

SWAIN M，1985. Communicative competence：some roles of
comprehensible input and comprehensible output in its development[M]//
GASS S，MADDEN C. Input in second language acquisition. London：
Newbury House.

SWAIN M，1995. Three functions of output in second language
learning[M]//COOK G，SEIDLHOFER B. Principles and practice in
applied linguistics：studies in honor of H.G. Widdowso. Oxford：Oxford
University Press.

TAGUCHI T，MAGID M，PAPI M，2009. The L2 motivational self system
among Japanese，Chinese and Iranian learners of English：a comparative

study[M]//DÖRNYEI Z, USHIODA E. Motivation, language identity and the L2 self. Bristol: Multilingual Matters.

THOMPSON S A, ERDIL-MOODY Z, 2014. Operationalizing multilingualism: language learning motivation in Turkey[J]. International journal of bilingual education and bilingualism, 19（3）: 314-331.

TREMBLAY P, GARDNER R C, 1995. Expanding the motivation construct in language learning[J]. Modern language journal, 79: 505-518.

UNSWORTH L, 2001. Teaching multiliteracies across the curriclum: changing contexts of text and image in classroom practice[M]. London: Open University Press.

VERA B, 2009. Motivation, language identity and the L2 self[M]// DÖRNYEI Z, USHIODA E. Bristol: Multilingual Matters.

VYGOTSKY L, 1978. Mind in society: the development of higher psychological processes[M]. Cambridge, MA: Harvard University Press.

WANG B, 2011. On the influential factors of the project-based English learning model upon learning motivation: a networked Neu-based empirical research [D]. Shanghai: Shanghai International Studies University.

WANG J, 2021. An exploration on an interactive teaching practice of College English listening courses based on Superstar learning platform[J]. English square, 7（2）: 21-23.

WANG X, DAI W D, 2015. Empirical study of two-language motivational strategy based on the "two-language motivational self-system" theory[J]. Foreign language teaching （6）: 48-52.

WEN Q F, 2008. Output-driven hypothesis and curriculum reform of English professional skills[J]. Foreign language （2）: 2-9.

WEN Q F, 2015. Building a theoretical system of production-oriented method[J]. Foreign language teaching and research （4）: 547-558.

WEN Q F, 2016. Teachers and students collaborative assessment: the new created evaluation form of POA[J]. Foreign language circles （5）: 37-43.

WEN Q F, 2017. The Chinese characteristics of POA[J]. Modern foreign language （3）: 348-358.

WILLIAMS M, BURDEN R L, 1997. Psychology for language teachers: a social constructivist approach[M]. Cambridge: Cambridge University Press.

WOO W H, 2016. Using Gagne's instructional model in phlebotomy education[J]. Advances in medical education & practice, 7: 511-516.

WU R H, HE G G, 2014. Application effect of cooperative learning in college English writing teaching[J]. Foreign language teaching, 35 （3）: 44-47.

WU X S, 2007. On the balance between reliability and validity of English test[J]. Journal of Guangxi university for nationalities （philosophy and social edition）, 29 （z2）: 129-130.

XIAO C, QIONG D, 2014. Empirical studies in university English teaching: take Tibet university for example[J]. Journal of Tibet university （social sciences edition）, 29 （3）: 169-176.

XU J F, CAO Z K, 2012. Empirical study of the effect of different pairing patterns on college English classroom students[J]. Chinese foreign language, 9 （5）: 67.

XU L, 2018. Construction of "SPOC + flipped classroom "ecosystem English teaching mode base on learners' demotivation[J]. Foreign language education, 39 （5）: 81-84, 89.

XU Z X, FENG X H, 2012. Empirical studies of motivational teaching strategies, English learning motivation, and the intrinsic structure of student classroom behavior[J]. Contemporary foreign language studies （8）: 5.

YANG L F, 2015. "New generation comprehensive college English course 2", the micro-lecture design of the "out-driven" link of POA, taking art and nature as an example[J]. Chinese foreign language education （4）: 3-9.

YANG T, LI L, 2010. Motivational process approach, self-system, and motivational strategy research[J]. Foreign language and foreign language teaching （5）: 62-67.

YANG X F, 2019. On the construction and influencing factors of SPOC-based college English teaching model[J]. Foreign language and literature （2）: 146-154.

YOU C J, 2010. A study of motivational strategies for high school English teachers[J]. Journal of the PLA foreign language institute （3）: 72-75.

YUAN P H, 2008. Research on the content-based foreign language teaching model in the English teaching environment of Chinese university [D]. Shanghai: Shanghai Jiao Tong University.

ZENG X Y, 2007. Analysis and illumination of motivation intensity of English learning of higher vocational students[J]. Vocational education research （6）: 115-116.

ZHANG D L, 2009. The application of multimodal speech theory and media technology in foreign language teaching[J]. Foreign language teaching, 30 （4）: 15-20.

ZHANG J, 2011. A study of hybrid audio-lingual model in college English teaching with the support of mobile technology[D]. Changchun: Northeast Normal University.

ZHANG K, ZHOU X M, YU C H, 2021. A meta-analysis of cooperative learning effect[J]. Journal of PLA university of foreign languages, 44 （4）: 95-104.

ZHANG L L, 2017. An experimental study on the effectiveness of the production-oriented approach[J]. Modern foreign languages, 40 （3）: 369-376.

ZHANG W J，2017. Applying production-oriented approach to college English teaching：an action research[D]. Beijing：Beijing Foreign Studies University.

ZHANG Y，2016. Research on the English teaching model under the CBI concept[J]. Modern education science （3）：65-69.

ZHAO N，WANG J J，2010. A study on classroom strategies for middle school English teachers[J]. Foreign language teaching theory and practice （1）：47-54.

ZHEN D S，1984. A brief discussion on the teaching mode and its management[J]. Tianjin normal university news （social science edition） （4）：34-35.

ZHENG H W，2004. Cooperative learning in college English teaching[J]. Zhanjiang （Lingnan） normal college journal，25（2）：112-114.

ZHONG M，2010. Combining inputs and outputs to facilitate student learning effectively[J]. Journal of southwest nationality university （humanities and social science），31（S1）：37-40.

ZHONG Z X，2006. Information technology teaching model[M]. Beijing：Beijing Normal University Press.

ZHU Y S，2007. Theoretical foundation and research methods for multimodal discourse analysis[J]. Foreign language journal （5）：82-86.

ZUO Y N，2018. Action research on college English writing based on production-oriented approach[J]. Journal of Honghe college，16（1）：4.

Appendices

Appendix A   The Chinese Version of the L2 Motivation Questionnaire (L2MQ)

亲爱的同学们，下面是关于你们外语学习动机的一些问题。请找出哪一个最准确地描述了你对下面问题的答案。如果你同意，请在左边的"符合"下标记圆圈。如果你不同意这个说法，请在右边的"不符合"下标记圆圈。问卷是匿名的，所以请不要把你的名字写在纸上。现在请阅读下面的句子。然后，选中一个最能描述你感觉的方框。

1= 非常符合；2= 符合；3= 有点符合；4= 不太符合；5= 不符合；6= 完全不符合

问题	1	2	3	4	5	6
我觉得英语课很无聊。我在英语课上总是感觉想睡觉						
我觉得这学期我的英语会取得进步						
我可以想象自己流利地写英语电子邮件或信件						
当我在英语课上发言时，我感到紧张和困惑						
我总是期待上英语课						
如果我努力的话，我想我能学好英语						

我可以想象自己住在国外，用英语进行讨论					
当我在英语课上不得不说英语时，我害怕同学会嘲笑我					
我很注意听老师在英语课上说的话					
我经常在英语课上体验到一种成功的感觉					
我可以想象自己在一所大学学习，在那里我所有的课程都是用英语教授的					
我总觉得其他学生的英语说得比我好					
我喜欢在英语课上说英语					
我相信有一天我的英语会说得很好					
我可以想象我和外国人说英语的情形					
我认为学英语很困难					
在英语课上，我通常知道该做什么和怎么做					
我可以想象自己和外国朋友或同事说英语					
每当我们有英语课时，我都很高兴					
我有信心在英语课上做演讲或陈述					
每当我想到我未来的职业生涯，我会想象自己用到英语					
我讨厌英语，但我别无选择。我只能坐在课堂上，别无选择					
我很担心自己不能学好英语					
我喜欢在课堂外也学习英语					
我经常在英语课上主动回答问题					
我宁愿把时间花在英语以外的科目上					

Appendix B   The English Version of the L2 Motivational Questionnaire (L2MQ) (in Categories)

Attitudes Toward the Course Section of the Questionnaire

1. I am looking forward to our English class.

2. I am attentive to what the teacher says in English class.

3. I like to speak English in English class.

4. I am very happy whenever we have English class.

5. I study English because I like it, not for the sake of passing exams or tests.

Linguistic Self-Confidence Section of the Questionnaire

1. I feel can make progress in English.

2. I think that I can learn English well, if I try hard enough.

3. I often experience a feeling of success in my English lessons.

4. I am sure that one day I will be able to speak English well.

5. In English lessons, I usually understand what to do and how to do it.

6. This semester, I think I will be good at learning English.

7. I often volunteer to answer questions in English lessons.

Ideal L2 Self

1. I can imagine myself writing English e-mails/letters fluently.

2. I can imagine myself living abroad and having a discussion in English.

3. I can imagine myself studying in a university where all my courses are taught in English.

4. I can imagine a situation where I am speaking English with foreigners.

5. I can imagine myself speaking English with international friends or colleagues.

6. Whenever I think of my future career, I imagine myself using English.

L2 Use Anxiety

1. I find English class very boring. I always feel sleepy in English class.

2. I get nervous and confused when I am speaking in my English class.

3. I am afraid that my classmates will laugh at me when I have to speak in English lessons.

4. I think it is very difficult to learn English.

5. I always feel that the other students speak English better than I do.

6. I hate English, but I have no choice. I just have to sit in class without any choice.

7. I am worried about my ability to do well in English.

8. I would rather spend time on subjects other than English.

Appendix C   Instruction for Students' Self-Reports

Write a reflection report on this semester's English teaching, including your overall feelings about this dynamic motivational teaching model, as well as your gains, problems and suggestions for future English class. You are required to write no less than 400 words.

Appendix D　Written Test Paper

Part Ⅰ　Writing (30minutes)

Directions: For this part, you are allowed 30 minutes to write a short essay about your view on the importance of physical exercise on campus. You should state the reasons and write at least 120 words but no more than 180 words.

Part Ⅱ　Listening Comprehension (25 minutes)
Section A

Directions: In this section, you will hear three news reports. At the end of each conversation, you will hear four questions. Both the news report and the questions will be spoken only once. After you hear a question, you must choose the best answer from the four choices marked A), B), C) and D). Then mark the corresponding letter on Answer Sheet 1 with a single line through the centre.

Questions 1 and 2 are based on the news report you have just heard.

1. A) An invention made by architects and engineers.

   B) A new device gathering information about buildings.

   C) An introduction of a three-dimensional model.

   D) New ways of building structures.

2. A) The accurate shape of rooms in the building.

   B) The size and position of heating and cooling equipment.

   C) The size and position of windows and doors.

   D) The placement of electrical outlets.

Questions 3 and 4 are based on the news report you have just heard.

3. A) Kids should spend more time outdoors.

   B) Kids all like trees and flowers.

   C) Kids may learn better in green nature.

   D) Kids should learn to protect nature.

4. A) They can distract a child's attention.

   B) They are easy to be accepted.

   C) They can hurt a child's health.

   D) They will affect a child's schooling.

Questions 5 to 7 are based on the news report you have just heard.

5. A) Permanent loss of eyesight of pilots.

   B) Loss of consciousness of passengers.

   C) Tragic results of air accidents.

   D) Blackouts of jet fighter pilots.

6. A) When the airplane slows down very quickly.

   B) When the airplane is making a sharp turn.

   C) When the pilots have a heart disease.

   D) When the pilots lose consciousness.

7. A) It is required by the laws and the government.

   B) The air pressure is rather low above the Earth's surface.

   C) The passengers will lose consciousness in the planes.

   D) Lack of oxygen can affect anyone at extreme heights.

Section B

Directions: In this section, you will hear two long conversations. At the end of each conversation, you will hear four questions. Both the conversation and the questions will be spoken only once. After you hear a question, you must choose the best answer from the four choices marked A), B), C), and D). Then mark the corresponding letter on Answer Sheet 1 with a single line through the centre.

Questions 8 to 11 are based on the conversation you have just heard.

8. A) Brentwood in America.   B) London.

    C) Essex in England.   D) Scotland.

9. A) It is a small town next to London.   B) It is a large population.

    C) It is in the southeast of Scotland.   D) It is a poor city.

10. A) It's a relatively small town.

    B) The people living there are very rich.

    C) Houses are scarce there.

    D) It's close to London.

11. A) The woman is not satisfied with the recreation there.

    B) The man thinks highly of the recreation there.

    C) All kinds of recreations are available there.

    D) The man thinks little of the recreation there.

Questions 12 to 15 are based on the conversation you have just heard.

12. A) He worked in a painting store.

    B) He worked in a painting factory.

    C) He worked in a gas stand.

    D) He worked in a bookstore.

13. A) To print the TV guides.

    B) To edit the TV guides.

    C) To sell the TV guides.

    D) To prepare the TV guides for distribution.

14. A) High pay and short work hours.

    B) Friendly environment and teamwork spirit.

    C) Relaxed atmosphere and valuable experience.

D) Good friends he made in the factory.

15. A) Delightful.　B) Meaningless.

C) Terrible.　D) Cruel.

Section C

Directions: In this section, you will hear three passages. At the end of each passage, you will hear some questions. Both the passage and the questions will be spoken only once. After you hear a question, you must choose the best answer from the four choices marked A), B), C) and D). Then mark the corresponding letter on Answer Sheet 1 with a single line through the centre.

Questions 16 to 18 are based on the passage you have just heard.

16. A) They think it looks like flowers.

B) They think it is full of passion.

C) They use it to show respect to Christ.

D) They think it is beautiful.

17. A) France.　B) The Caribbean.

C) England.　D) Canada.

18. A) It is about the size of an egg.　B) It is with a brown skin.

C) It is full of yellow seeds.　D) It is about the size of an orange.

Questions 19 to 21 are based on the passage you have just heard.

19. A) A book.　B) A clock.

C) A shirt.　D) A suitcase.

20. A) Fastening her seat belts.

B) Listening to the music.

C) Enjoying the beauty of the evening sky.

D) Sitting in a smoke filled room.

21. A) She lost her ticket.

B) She was thought bringing a time bomb.

C) She made some mistakes.

215

D) She passport had some problems.

Questions 22 to 25 are based on the passage you have just heard.

22. A) They have unwritten regulations.

B) They never punish the violators.

C) They have the promising prospects.

D) They have strict rules.

23. A) He will be perceived as a successful person.

B) He will be less likely to get promotion.

C) He will be more successful.

D) He will be pushed aside by his colleagues.

24. A) Try to modify it.   B) Criticize it directly.

C) Don't judge it.   D) Shoot it down.

25. A) He who creates the idea deserves the credit himself.

B) It doesn't matter if a business owner borrows his employee's idea.

C) You can borrow other people's idea if you work as a team.

D) The victim will forget soon if you borrow his idea.

Part Ⅲ Reading Comprehension (40 minutes)

Section A

Directions: In this section, there is a passage with ten blanks. You are required to select one word for each blank from a list of choices given in a word bank following the passage. Read the passage through carefully before making your choices. Each choice in the bank is identified by a letter. Please mark the corresponding letter for each item on Answer Sheet 2 with a single line through the centre. You may not use any of the words in the bank more than once.

Questions 26 to 35 are based on the following passage.

Education makes our lives richer. It __26__ us with opportunities. So the amount that girls were allowed to __27__ in education is an important part of

American history. Women's participation as teachers is an important part of history, too.

In Colonial times, school was __28__ for boys; it was usually taught by a young man, since parents felt that boys needed __29__ leadership.

In the 19th century, more women became school teachers. These teachers were often very young women, even __30__. Usually, they taught for only a few years. By about the 1840s, teaching had become a women's profession. Now people wanted a teacher who would __31__ and support their children, not a strict school master. They felt that women were more __32__ to the job. By the 1850s nearly all teachers were women, especially in the elementary schools. Still, not all girls __33__ school, and schools still focused mainly on educating boys. This began to change by the end of the 19th century when our country decided that all children should have free __34__ education. However, it did not happen right away; at first, schools still focused on the boys as they had in the past.

During the 20th century, the majority of children, both boys and girls, attended school regularly. The teaching __35__ continued to be made up mostly of women. Since the 1930s, about 70% of the teaching force has been women.

A) attended	I) profession
B) completely	J) provides
C) mainly	K) public
D) mild	L) scold
E) nurture	M) strict
F) offers	N) suited
G) participate	O) teenagers
H) private	

Section B

Directions: In this section, you are going to read a passage with ten statements attached to it. Each statement contains information given in one of the paragraphs. Identify the paragraph from which the information is derived. You may choose a paragraph more than once. Each paragraph is marked with a letter. Answer the questions by marking the corresponding letter on Answer Sheet 2.

Testing Baby's Brain

[A] As far as her friends and teachers are concerned, Ashdod is an ordinary, bright, playful 5-year-old girl. They might be surprised to learn that not long ago therapists (治疗专家) were fighting to keep her from suffering from autism (孤独症)—a brain disorder that afflicts one in 100 children, typically leaving them with lifelong difficulties in communicating, socializing and carrying out many basic tasks. Ashdod was lucky; when she was 10 months old, her parents became alarmed that she had little interest in looking them in the eyes, waiting and moving from her back, and took her to the Mifne Center in Rosh Pinna, Israel, a clinic that focuses on children 5 months and older who show early warning signs of autism. The results of the Mifne treatment were shocking, recalls the girl's mother, Tikva. "Now she goes to a regular school where she is the same sort of active, funny, normal child as anyone else, " she says.

[B] Despite a big jump in autism awareness in the past decade, parents, schools and doctors still frequently ignore warning signs in very young children. These can be difficult to detect: a child never points at things, shows more interest in objects than people, has delayed speech and develops a fascination with toys turning around. Many experts regard these symptoms as harmless habits that kids will outgrow. New research and experience in some autism clinics, however, suggests that staring treatment by age 2 is critical to mitigating and in some cases entirely avoiding the disorder.

[C] That's because unlike the brain of an adult or even an older child, a 12- or 18-month-old's brain is, in a sense, highly reprogrammable—that is, it responds well to treatments designed to permanently change basic patterns of thought and behavior. "All the evidence we have suggests that outcomes for these children will be better with an earlier diagnosis(诊断), before they reach 18 months, if possible," says Christopher Gillberg, a professor at Gothenburg University in Sweden.

[D] Although there are currently no effective treatments for autism symptoms in older children or adults, the prospects are turning out to be entirely different for very young children who get prompt treatment. Psychologists have had remarkable success with behavioral therapy, which involves therapists working intensively with children to get them to do tasks they're having difficulty with. The Mifne Center in Israel applies its own form of intensive therapy, typically lasting about two weeks and focusing on getting the child to make contact with parents and to eat and move normally. Some 200 children have been through the program; about three quarters have remained free of any signs of autism or any other significant developmental disorder, according to Mifne founder and director Hanna Alonim. "If we can get them here as babies, close to 100 percent won't develop autism," she says. "If we don't see them until they're 2, it's a different story." To support Mifne's findings with more-formal research, doctors at the Tel Aviv Sourasky Medical Center have begun screening and videotaping infants thought to be at risk of pre-autism before the Mifne treatment.

[E] Having a treatment choice for infants raises the hard issue of diagnosis. Autism can be tricky to recognize—it encompasses any or all of a broad range of symptoms, including difficulty with social interactions, language, motor skills and taking in sensory information, as well as repetitive behaviors, eating problems and in some cases unusually high or low levels of activity. A study of nearly 10,000 children in Bergen, Norway, indicated that the number of children who showed "pronounced autistic features" was about five times higher than the number who qualified for a formal diagnosis of autism.

[F] Even children who exhibit only partial or mild versions of autism symptoms are at risk of ending up with lifelong challenges, say researchers, and would benefit from autism therapies. But tagging more very young children as candidates for autism therapy creates another problem. The cost of behavioral therapy is eye-open in applied behavior analysis, an intensive treatment that requires 15-to-25 hours of sessions a week, costs about $30,000 a year, and even a modest program typically runs about $10,000 a year. That's one reason studies estimate that less than one in 10 very young children with a diagnosis of autism get 25 hours a week of therapy.

[G] Health-care systems are not up to this task. In the United States, where health insurance rarely covers such treatments, the chances of having the government pay for therapy varies wildly from state to state. Children don't necessarily fare much better under national health care. The United Kingdom pays for treatment—but often only after the parents hire a lawyer and win their case at a regional "tribunal", where more often than not communities will fight to force the parents to settle for the few hours a week of therapy offered in a local special-education program. In Italy, toddlers with disorders who love near large cities in the north-central part of the country can get the attention of a team of therapists, but those in the southern, rural areas tend to get few services. Laurence Robel, a child psychiatrist and autism researcher at the Necker Children's Hospital in Paris, notes that France keeps a bias against behavioral therapy, which critics compare to training a dog or programming a robot. "Away from Paris," she says, "children are lucky to receive much treatment at all."

[H] Experts insist that governments are being penny-wise and pound-foolish in refusing to pony (付清) up for intensive therapy to infants and toddlers who show early signs of a developmental disorder. Simple, brief screening tests are now designed to flag children at risk as early as 18 months. Earlier diagnosis might be possible by measuring brain activity and recognizing patterns that are unique to autism. Researchers at the Baby Lab in Uppsala University in Sweden are looking for these patterns by placing dozens of soft-foam sensors on infant's heads.

[I] The benefits of early treatment are likely to grow in coming years as new research into developmental disorders continues to pay off.

36. In Italy, the chances for young children to receive services of a team of autism therapists vary between the north-central part of the country and the southern, rural areas.

37. In detecting the warning signs of autism in young children, parents, schools and doctors now haven't done sufficiently on it.

38. Autism is not easy to recognize because it covers a wide range of symptoms.

39. It is very important to treat a child with autism by age of two, because children at that age respond well to the related treatment.

40. According to the text, children who get autism may suffer from troubles in communicating.

41. It is an effective treatment for older children with signs of autism to ask them to do tasks which are difficult for them.

42. According to experts, those governments are extremely foolish if they refuse to support the intensive therapy to young children showing early signs of a developmental disorder.

43. Most very young children with a diagnosis of autism do not have an intensive treatment, because it's too expensive to receive the intensive treatment.

44. About 150 children have recovered from signs of autism in the Mifne

Center.

45. In the United States, different state governments pay differently for autism therapy because health insurance rarely covers such treatments.

Section C

Directions: There are 2 passages in this section. Each passage is followed by some questions or unfinished statements. For each of them there are four choices marked A), B), C) and D). You should decide on the best choice and mark the corresponding letter on Answer Sheet 2 with a single line through the centre.

Passage One

Questions 46 to 50 are based on the following passage.

What should you think about in trying to find your career? You are probably better at some school subjects than others. These may show strengths that you can use in your work. A boy who is good at mathematics can use that in an engineering career. A girl who spells well and likes English may be good at office work. So it is important to know the subjects you do well in at school. On the other hand, you may not have any specially strong or weak subjects but your records show a general satisfactory standard. Although not all subjects can be used directly in a job, they may have indirect value. A knowledge of history is not required for most jobs but if history is one of your good subjects you will have learned to remember facts and details. This is an ability that can be useful in many jobs.

Your school may have taught you skills, such as typing or technical drawing, which you can use in your work. You may be good at metal work or cookery and look for a job where you can improve these skills. If you have had a part-time job on Saturdays or in the summer, think about what you gained from it. If nothing else, you may have learned how to get to work on time, to follow instructions and to get on with older workers. You may have learned to give correct change in a shop, for example, just as important; you may become interested in a particular industry or career you see from the inside in a pare-time job.

Facing your weak points is also part of knowing yourself. You may be all thumbs when you handle tools, and perhaps you are a poor speller or cannot add up to a column of figures. It is better to face any weaknesses than to pretend they do not exist. Your school record, for instance, may not be too good, yet it is an important part of your background. You should not be apologetic about it but instead recognize that you will have a chance of a fresh start at work.

46. Which of the following can best sum up the first paragraph?

A) The importance of doing well at school.

B) Using school performance to help to choose a career.

C) The importance of being good at all subjects.

D) The indirect value of school work.

47. The subject which is supposed to have no direct value for job hunting is_____.

A) mathematics   B) English

C) technical drawing   D) history

48. The writer thinks that for a student to have a part-time job is probably_____.

A) a waste of time that could have been spent on study

B) useful for his future work

C) a good way to earn extra money

D) a good way to find out his weak points

49. According to the passage, if a student's school record is not good, he_____.

A) will fail in his future work

B) will not be able to find a suitable jib

C) will regret not having worked harder at school

D) may do well in his future work

50. The whole passage centers on ＿＿＿＿.

A) choosing a career according to what one is good at

B) acquiring knowledge by working hard at school

C) finding one's strong and weak points

D) developing one's abilities in school work

Passage Two

Questions 51 to 55 are based on the following passage.

Drink from plastic bottles can raise the body's levels of a controversial "gendeer-bending" chemical by more than two thirds, according to tests.

Experts have been concerned about the possible health effects of bisphenol A (BPA)—an everyday chemical used in many plastic food and drink containers and tins as well as clear baby bottles—which is officially classified as toxic in some countries.

A study found that participants who drank for a week from polycarbonate (聚碳酸酯) bottles showed a 69 percent increase in their urine of BPA.

Researchers did not say how much liquid was drunk per day. Researchers from Harvard School of Public Health studied 77 students, who had first undergone a seven-day "washout" phase in which they drank all cold beverages from stainless steel bottles in order to minimise BPA exposure.

They were then given two polycarbonate bottles and asked to drink all cold beverages from them during the week. Previous studies have suggested that high levels of BPA consumption are linked to birth defects, growth problems and an increased risk of heart disease. In particular there are fears that heating the bottles, as parents would do when warming their baby's milk, causes the chemical to leak in potentially dangerous quantities into the liquid contained within.

"If you heat those bottles, as is the case with baby bottles, we would expect the levels to be considerably higher. This would be of concern since infants may be particularly susceptible to BPA's hormone gland-disrupting (扰乱腺体激素分泌) potential." said the senior author of the latest study, Karin B. Michels.

Most adults carry BPA in their bodies but expert opinion on the risks is divided. The European Food Safety Authority believes that people naturally convert the chemical into less harmful substances in the body.

Previous studies had found that BPA could leach from polycarbonate bottles into their contents, but this study is the first to show the size of the corresponding increase in urinary BPA concentrations in humans.

Harvard researcher Jenny Carwile said, "While previous studies have demonstrated that BPA is linked to adverse health effects, this study fills in a missing piece of the puzzle—whether or not polycarbonate plastic bottles are an important contributor to the amount of BPA in the body."

51. What can we know about bisphenol A (BPA) from the beginning of the passage?

A) It is certain substance taken in by human beings every day.

B) It is a component contained in a number of plastic products.

C) It is an element that plays a decisive role in people's gender.

D) It is a kind of chemical that is universally regarded poisonous.

52. According to Paragraph 4, the "washout" phase was designed to_____.

A) make the research be accomplished with a result as satisfying as possible

B) obtain references for the possible health effects of stainless steel bottles

C) eliminate substances in bodies that may affect the result of the research

D) limit the sort of beverages taken in by participants to the minimum level

53. What result can be expected if baby bottles containing polycarbonate

are heated?

A) The liquid in the bottles would absorb limited amount of converted BPA.

B) The infants should be seriously bothered by such disease as heart attack.

C) Babies would consume more BPA if they drink the liquid in the bottles.

D) The infants would undoubtedly refuse to drink the liquid in the bottles.

54. How do experts evaluate the hazard that can be caused by BPA?

A) They think it is so common in bodies that it isn't hazardous material.

B) Different groups hold different viewpoints on this issue.

C) They believe it will be transformed into other safe materials.

D) They consider the amount of BPA in bodies decides its harmfulness.

55. What is the significance of the study talked about in this passage?

A) It proved the assumption on BPA that studied previously.

B) It clarified the high risks that BPA may pose to people's health.

C) It confirmed the principal source of the substance BPA.

D) It showed what's responsible for the rising level of BPA in humans.

Part IV Translation (30 minutes)

Directions: For this part, you are allowed 30 minutes to translate a passage from Chinese into English. You should write your answer on Answer Sheet 2.

随着中国经济的快速发展和国际交往的日益广泛，世界各国对汉语学习的需求急剧增长。在借鉴其他国家推广本民族语言经验的基础上，中国从2004 年起开始在海外设立孔子学院。孔子学院是以教授汉语和传播中国文化为宗旨的非营利（non-profit）机构。到 2012 年年底，中国已经在全球108 个国家和地区建立了大约 400 所孔子学院和 50 个孔子课堂。

Appendix E Oral Test

PART 1 Interview

Examiner: Now, in this first part, I'd like to ask you some more questions about yourself, OK? Let's talk about friends.

How often do you spend time with your friends?

What type of things do you and your friends do together?

What kinds of things do you do to show you are a good friend?

Would you prefer to have a lot of acquaintance or a few good friends? (And why?)

PART 2 Individual Long Turn

Examiner: Now, I'm going to give you a topic and I'd like you to talk about it for one to two minutes. Before you talk, you'll have one minute to think about what you're going to say. You can make some notes if you wish. Do you understand?

I'd like you to describe someone in your family who you like.

You should say the following:

How this person is related to you?

What this person look like?

What kind of person he/she is?

And why do you like this person?

PART 3 Two-Way Discussion

Examiner: We've been talking about family members, and now I'd like to discuss with you further.

In what ways can people in a family be similar to each other?

Do you think that daughters are always more similar to mothers than to male relatives? Why? What about sons and fathers?

In terms of personality, are people more influenced by their family or by friends? In what ways?

Appendix F Scoring Criterion for Writing and Translation in Written Test Paper

Scoring Criterion for Writing

The composition of CET-4 adopts the general impression scoring. The full score is 15, dividing into five bands: 14 (13–15), 11 (10–12), 8 (7–9), 5 (4–6) and 2 (1–3). Each band is described as follows:

Band	Band descriptions
14	•Address the task pertinently. •Present a fully developed position with relevant and well supported ideas. •Use cohesion with very natural control of lexical features. •Use a wide range of vocabulary fluently with rare minor errors occur only as "slips".
11	•Address the task relevantly. •Present a well-developed response to the question with relevant and supported ideas. •Sequence information and ideas logically. •Make occasional errors in spelling and/or word formation.
8	•Address basically relevant to the topic, but there are some places that are not expressed clearly. • Present information with some organization but there may be a lack of overall progression. • Make use of cohesive device in a limited way. • May make noticeable errors in spelling and/or word formation that may cause some difficulty for the reader.
5	•Address the task only partially. •Express ideas inaccurately. •Have little control of organizational features. •Language errors predominate and may cause strain for the reader.
2	•Answer is completely unrelated to the task. •Fail to communicate any message. •Can use only a few isolated words. •Cannot use sentences forms at all.

Scoring criterion for translation

As with the composition, the CET-4 translation also adopts the overall impression scoring method. The full mark is 15, consisting five bands:14 (13–15), 11 (10–12), 8 (7–9), 5 (4–6) and 2 (1–3). Each band is described as follows:

Band	Band description
14	•Express the meaning accurately. •The translation is fluent with a clear structure. •The words are appropriate, basically no language errors, only a few slips.
11	•Basically express the meaning of the original text. •The structure is moderately clear. •The language is smooth, but there are a few language errors.
8	• Expresses the meaning of the original text in a limited way. •The translation is constrainedly coherent. •There are quite a lot of language errors, some of which are serious mistakes.
5	•Only express the meaning of a small part of the original text. •The translation is inconsistent. •Have a considerable number of serious language errors.
2	•Except for individual words or sentences, the translation basically does not express the meaning of the original text.

Appendix G   A Model Teaching Plan for the Experimental Group

This is a sample showing how this dynamic motivational teaching model in the Chinese college English context is implemented in the course content, and the material chosen is Unit 1 "Growing Up" from New College English Book 1. This unit consists of two texts with the same theme of the difficult and rewarding experience of growing up. Based on the unit productive task, the teaching focuses on the first text "Writing for Myself", which is a typical narration with a complete narrative structure, especially the good use of its selecting details to support the author's point, making the story vivid and touching. It is a well written narrative work, and there are a lot of writing skills worth students learning. The unit productive task has been designed to ask students to present a speech with the theme of growing up, according to which, the learning objectives are the following:

1. Identify and use the six elements of storytelling in writing;

2. Identify and use detailed description in writing;

3. Enable the students to express themselves freely on the theme of "Growing Up";

4. Present a speech about growing up.

A Sample of Teaching Plan

Teaching procedure	Teaching content	Cooperative learning	Multimodality	Motivational strategies
Motivating & Enabling Periods 1&2	Before the class, the teacher releases the unit productive task: Growing up is not easy, and there must be someone who has played a big role and left deep impression on you. Our university is going to organize an English-speaking contest on the topic "The one who has the most influence on me as I grow up". You plan to give a presentation, state what this person did or said that had a good influence on the shaping of your character, behavior or attitude.	Students discussed in group and then evaluate the output of their peers for the first time according to a detailed persuasive speech.	The teacher releases the task in the form of mini-lecture online.	Make the teaching materials and the unit task relevant to the students by relating the subject matter to everyday experiences and backgrounds of the learners. Make sure that they know exactly that success in the task involves.
	Students are required to watch a mini-lecture online to learn the background information, vocabulary and structure of the text, and then the teacher gives a test to students online on important language points in the text, then the teacher discusses with students the key and difficult points in online courses and answer questions.	Interaction between teacher and students online	Video (mini-lecture)	• Increase the learners' expectancy of success in particular tasks by providing sufficient preparation and offering assistance. • Increase the students' motivation by actively promoting learner autonomy.

Motivating & Enabling Periods 1&2	Step1: In class, the teacher checks students' first attempt of the unit production task.	/	Speech	Make learning stimulating by making task challenging.
	Step 2: The teacher introduces the teaching objectives and divides the unit production task into three sub-tasks: a. An interview: Who is he or she? What is he or she like? b. Narration writing: your experience with him or her that led to the change in your attitude toward life, study or friendship. c. Speech: The person who has the most influence on you as you grow up.	The sub-tasks have to be finished by pair or group cooperation.	The sub-tasks are in both oral and written form.	Make task content attractive by including novelty and variety.
	Step 3: The teacher plays a video about a super star who talks about the people who have made a difference in their life.	Students watch the video, and work in group to share their ideas which can be conducive to their views of the production task.	Video	Increase the learners' expectancy of success in particular tasks by providing sufficient preparation and offering assistance.
	Step 4: The teacher asks students to scan the text and find out all the language describing the image of Mr. Fleagle, his former English teacher. Then, the teacher guides students to summarize the expression of the description of people.	/	PPT	The same as above.

Motivating & Enabling Periods 1&2	Step 5: Student role-play an interview to talk and describe the image and as well as their feeling about this person.	Work in pair	Task in oral mode	Make learning stimulating and enjoyable by creating specific roles and enlisting them as active task participants.
Enabling Periods 3&4	Step1: The teacher explains the six elements that make up the narrative: when, where, who, what, why, how.	Students listen individually	PPT	/
	Step 2: The teacher asks each group of students to browse the text in 5 minutes, and asks the students to find out the background, characters and narrative perspective in the story. Step 3: The teacher asks the students to read the text again, understand the plot of the story, and to find out the various scenes in the story, including beginning, development, climax, ending.	Students complete Story Map in group. Students describe each scene briefly on Story Map 2 in group.	The teacher displays the work of each group of students on the screen through E-learning APP.	Promote interaction, cooperation by including information-gap activities for which students pair up to cooperatively complete a meaningful and challenging task.

	After the class, students are required to read and identify the narrative elements in "The Red Jacket" (Text B), and to finish the second sub-task: narration writing with six elements of narration included.	After finishing their assignment independently, students submit them in group, and are encouraged to upload online as early as possible, because the last group submitting have to entertain the whole class by giving performance the next class.	Task in written form Submit via online learning platform.	Increase students' goal-orientedness by drawing students' attention from time to time to unit goals. Take into account team products and not just individual products in your assessments. Make task attractive by including novel, intriguing, authentic, humorous, competitive.
Enabling Periods 3&4	Step 1: Ask students to make an evaluation of a student work with problems shared by a majority of students, then the teacher introduces the use of details in the text to support the author's point as well as the use of transitional words to make a story well connected. Guide students to identify the detailed description in the text as well as in the reading materials prepared by the teacher as a complement.	Students first evaluate individually and then make a group discussion. The group work together to find out the detailed description.	PPT Text	• Provide regular feedbacks about the progress your students are making and about the areas which they should particularly concentrate on. • Include problem-solving activities that lead to the successful completion of whole-group tasks or involve small-group tasks. •Teach students learning strategies to facilitate the intake of new materials.
	Step 3: Ask students to revise the draft and adapt the story into a speech, requiring the use of detailed description and cohesion device.	Work in pair	/	Make sure that they know exactly that success in the task involves.
Assessing Periods 7&8	Before class, the teacher browses the second draft submitted by students, and determine the focus of evaluation: how to avoid run-on sentences.	/	Online	Provide regular feedbacks about the progress your students are making and about the areas which they should particularly concentrate on.

Assessing Periods 7&8	Step 1: In class the teacher asks students to do sample analysis of students' revised draft, first the well written sample followed by the deficient one or two to be improved, including: predicate verbs used together and run-on sentence.	Students were guided to evaluate samples independently according to the assessment criterion set by the teacher, then students carried out group discussions.	The teacher presents 2–3 students' samples through PPT.	Protect the learners' self-esteem and increase their self-confidence by providing learners with regular experiences of success, teaching them various learners strategies.
	Step 2: The teacher gives the revised opinions prepared in advance, which is turning multiple simple sentences into (a) compound sentence, (b) subordinate clause, (c) use the non-predicate verb, then asks students to rate peer's composition and give advice.	Work in pair	PPT	Increase the learners' expectancy of success in particular tasks by providing sufficient preparation and offering assistance.
	Step 3: One student from each group is chosen to give a speech in class, and the teacher and students evaluate students' stage presentation according to assessment criteria.	Work in pair and group	/	• Encourage pairs or groups report their task to the whole class to check comprehension and accuracy. • Make the assessment system completely transparent and incorporate mechanisms by which the learners and their peers can also express their views.
	After class, students self-evaluate their second draft and performance, and then recorded video and submit it to the online learning platform.	Work in pair	E-learning APP	/

Appendix H   A Model Teaching Plan for the Control Group

I   Objectives

Grasp the main idea and structure of the text (narration in chronological sequence);

Appreciate the narrative skills demonstrated in the text (selection of details, repetition, coherence.);

Master the key language points and grammatical structures in the text;

Conduct a series of reading, listening, speaking and writing activities related to the theme of the unit.

II   Time Allotment

Periods 1–2	Periods 3–4	Periods 5–6	Periods 7–8
Pre-reading; While-reading (Text structure, cultural notes, language points)	While-reading (Language points)	While-reading (Language points, grammatical structures)	Post-reading (Check on students' exercises and home reading (Text B)

III Teaching Procedure

1. Pre-Reading

1) Warm-up Activity

The teacher asks students to listen to John Lennon's *Beautiful Boy* and then asks students questions:

—What does Lennon think of growing up?

—What do you think of growing up? Is it easy or full of adventures?

—Do you have any memorable experience in your growing up?

2) Lead-in to Text A, "Writing for Myself", T asks Ss the following questions:

—Would you enjoy writing "The Art of Eating Spaghetti"? Why or why not?

—Why did Russell Baker enjoy writing "The Art of Eating Spaghetti"? (Hint: Para. 4)

—Look at the title of Text A, then find out in which paragraph a similar phrase appears. Read that paragraph carefully and explain in your own words what the author means by saying "write for myself". (Hint: Para.5)

3) T explains to Ss cultural background information occurring in the text, including: the art of eating Spaghetti, the U.S. grade school system and how school teachers are dressed.

2. While-Reading

1) Grasping the structure of the text

(1) Ss circle all the time words, phrases and clauses in Text A. When they finish, T asks several Ss to read aloud what they have circled.

(2) T draws Ss' attention to Organization Exercise 2, reads its instructions, and asks them these two questions:

—Refer to the time words/phrases/clauses you have just circled and tell from which point on Baker starts talking about his new experience.

—Starting from which paragraph does Baker stop writing about his new experience? (Hint: the paragraph containing "when I finished" and "next morning".)

a. In this way Ss will be able to divide the text into 3 parts and sum up the main idea.

b. Several Ss report the main idea they have summed up to the class.

2) T explains language points and gives Ss practice.

3) Grammatical structures

(1) T asks Ss to form pairs and ask each other questions based on Para. 2 using the structure "sb./sth. is said/believed/reported to do/be". T may offer the following model:

—What kind of person is Mr. Fleagle?

—He was said/reported/believed to be very formal, rigid and hopelessly out-of-date.

Afterwards, a pair or two may repeat their questions and answers to the class.

(2) Ss do Structure Exercise 2 in the textbook.

4) T draws Ss' attention to writing strategy in theme-related language learning tasks, especially the part about details. T then asks the following questions:

—In Part 1, what details are selected to show "I'd been bored with everything associated with English courses"?

—In Part 1, what details are given to show that Mr. Fleagle was dull and rigid?

—In Part 2, which sentences show that at first Baker was unwilling to write the essay?

—In Part 3, the author didn't tell us directly that his essay was very good. By which sentences did he manage to give us the impression that his essay was very good?

5) Synonymous words or phrases in this text:

(1) T chooses one word from each group of synonyms listed in Text Analysis, and asks Ss to scan for respective synonyms. If Ss' findings are inconclusive, T may reveal those they have neglected.

(2) T may further provoke Ss' thinking by this question: Why does Russell Baker employ all these synonymous words and phrases?

6) When T and Ss come to the sentence "In the eleventh grade, at the eleventh hour as it were, I had discovered a calling" in Para. 9, T may ask Ss to recall a similar sentence they have read. (Para.1, "The idea of becoming a writer had come to me off and on since my childhood in Belleville, but it wasn't until my third year in high school that the possibility took hold.") By this T will show Ss the importance of coherence in writing.

3. After Reading

1) Think alone: According to Mr. Fleagle, what is the very essence of the essay?

Then T invites several Ss to give their opinions. T may sum up by this sentence—"The essence of good essay is to write what one enjoys writing about".

2) T checks if Ss have done the rest of the after-text exercises in their spare time, and discusses some common errors that crop up.

Acknowledgements

The whole process of composing this book is both a precious and challenging experience to me. Fortunately, I have so many amazing people on my side who have supported, encouraged, and inspired me.

First and foremost, my deepest gratitude goes to my supervisor, Dr. Ngamthip Wimolkasem, who has devoted her time, effort, support and help that I needed to complete such a huge task. I truly feel blessed and privileged to be her student and advisee. Dr. Ngamthip Wimolkasem has walked me through all the stages of the composing the book, and many of the ideas grew out of repeated interactions with her. I was often amazed at her efficiency in her proofreading of my work, and admired her ability in focusing on the overall research design globally, and at the same time, attending to the fine points in the study. It can be said that without her insightful suggestions, illuminating comments, consistent guidance, this book could not have reached its present fruitful state.

Second, I also would like to express my heartful thanks to Dr. Suwattana Eamoraphan, Dr. Joseph Foley, Dr. Marilyn Deocampo, and Dr. Kulaporn Hiranburana in Assumption University, for teaching me and helping me to cultivate my basic academic literacy, and laying the foundation for my research and writing, and also to Dr. Supong Tangkiengsirisin and Dr. Prannapha Modehiran for their kindness in coming to my research proposal presentation and giving me the previous and insightful advice to improve my book.

Third, I owe my sincere gratitude to my doctoral classmates and friends, Li Xinying, Cui Han and Zhao Jing, for their great friendship, companion and generosity, who made my study abroad an enjoyable and forgettable experience. I also wish to express my thankfulness to the students participating in this study. They are full of vigor and enthusiasm, and they have made a sincere and pertinent evaluation of my teaching, and provided data support for my research. Many thanks also go to my colleague, Ning Zhongnian and Yang Xiaoli for their cooperation when I conducted my experiment teaching and also for their helping me score the participants' tests and other selfless assistance.

Finally, my special obliges go to my family who have given me a great support in the course of pursuing my doctor degree. My mother-in-law helped me take care of my baby I delivered during the period, and without her devotion and support, I could never have concentrated on study with all my heart. My beloved husband has taken the responsibility of my elder child's education, and has always been there whenever I need him, especially when I feel confused and frustrated, he has always been a good listener and always provided his encouragement and emotional support to me. Thank you!